Multiprofessional Com

Multiprofessional Communication

Making Systems Work for Children

Georgina Glenny and
Caroline Roaf

 Open University Press

Open University Press
McGraw-Hill Education
McGraw-Hill House
Shoppenhangers Road
Maidenhead
Berkshire
England
SL6 2QL

email: enquiries@openup.co.uk
world wide web: www.openup.co.uk

and Two Penn Plaza, New York, NY 10121-2289, USA

First published 2008

A catalogue record of this book is available from the British Library

ISBN-10: 0 335 22856 9 (pb)   0 335 22855 0 (Hb)
ISBN-13: 978 0 335 22856 0 (pb)   978 0 335 22855 3 (Hb)

Library of Congress Cataloguing-in-Publication Data
CIP data applied for

Typeset by BookEns Ltd, Royston, Herts.
Printed in Great Britain by Bell and Bain Ltd., Glasgow

The McGraw·Hill Companies

Contents

List of figures and tables

Figures

Tables

Acknowledgements

This book has only been possible because of the generous cooperation of all the field workers, parents and children who have contributed to the research and to whom we owe our first thanks. We would also like to acknowledge the work of Pat Goodwin who first drew our attention to the significance of local networks in the overall pattern of provision and to her modelling of the system minder role in the context of mental health provision. We are especially grateful to Jane Harrison and Gloria Walker for a deeper understanding of how the role can be developed in relation to children and young people. None of this work would have been possible without the support of our funders, the Calouste Gulbenkian Foundation, the Hamilton Trust, the Oxfordshire Children's Fund and Oxfordshire Local Authority.

1 Introduction: the challenge of multiprofessional working

'Better multiprofessional working' has been the remedy of choice in many reviews of services to support vulnerable children and young people. Yet outside the realms of tightly focused specialist teams it seems to have been very difficult to achieve the lasting benefits for children and young people expected of it.

Huxham and Vangen (2005), documenting a range of different types of partnership over the last 15 years, stress the difficulties and the energy it can take to achieve successful collaboration, and counsel caution. They observed that many attempts at partnership produced what they described as *collaborative inertia*, that is, the gains from the collaborative activity did not justify the time taken in developing and sustaining the partnership and thus resulted in disappointment and frustration. They concluded that in order to achieve *collaborative advantage* collaboration should only take place when absolutely necessary and, to be successful, an ongoing commitment to the processes that underpin effective collaboration has to be made: 'the nurturing process must be continuous and permanent' (p. 75).

For children's services to function effectively to meet the needs of vulnerable children and young people, collaboration has indeed come to be regarded as essential in Huxham and Vangen's sense. In 1997, as a result of the groundswell of opinion developed in the previous two decades and especially since the publication of the 1989 Children Act and, more recently, the Laming Report (2003), the newly elected Labour government formally recognized this need and set about addressing it with considerable verve and imagination. The new climate of support for interagency collaboration led Roaf (2002), documenting the policy background since the Beveridge Report of 1942, to observe that 'The practice of inter-agency work is now [i.e. post 1997] at a transition stage. Having been associated for some years with usually small-scale, short term local projects, inter-agency practice is now developing rapidly in response to the setting up of large scale government supported initiatives' (p. 6).

While it was undoubtedly a significant sign of progress to reconfigure previously distinct children's services into a single agency, there was likely to be continued discussion, not to say dissent, about how the development from small- to large-scale collaboration would be achieved in practice both locally and nationally. At the very least, newly reconfigured services would be exposed to the unpredictability of politics. The government's endorsement of multiprofessional working was welcomed but there were few illusions about either the complexity of the task or the questions which would then be raised. How radical could local authorities and national government be? What shape would the new agencies take? How easy would it be to evaluate the effect of the new way of working?

Learning from the margins

There was also the question of how links were to be made and maintained with other agencies, housing for example, with which strong links would be required but which would not necessarily be appropriately gathered under one roof. At that time Roaf (2002) concluded that 'No matter how agencies group or regroup, the need for co-operation remains and without it clients are no more likely to receive a co-ordinated response from agencies than they were a generation ago' (p. 32). In other words, the reconfiguration of services has revealed that boundaries, in relation to children and young people, are a constant. In addition, the desire to dissolve boundaries might in fact distract from the more fundamental work of learning both how to negotiate them and from what goes on there. The new silo, created to break down the old pattern, remains a silo, albeit more diverse. The observations and judgements made at its margins provide the critically important feedback policy makers need in order to improve the functioning of the whole system. Multiprofessional collaboration, in whatever form it takes, can only achieve what is expected of it in terms of improved practice in the light of this understanding.

At this point it is worth going back a step to reflect on what the pioneers of multiprofessional practice were actually doing when they set up their innovative projects in a context of what was then considerable professional and political resistance to the concept of large-scale interagency collaboration. In general, these projects were small scale, for example Gulaboff (1989), Exeter Youth Support Team (1992), Surrey County Council (1992), Roaf and Lloyd (1995). However, Scotland had already, in the early 1990s, embarked on some larger-scale interagency collaboration as evidenced by, for example, Mapstone's classic study *Crossing the Boundaries* (1983) and the development of youth strategy in Lothian and Strathclyde (Maginnis 1989; Russell 1989). The practitioners in these projects and studies invariably started from where their clients were and thought outside the box, connecting for support and inspiration with all those in their localities whose work impinged on the group whose difficulties they sought to alleviate.

Interestingly, the notion that matters would improve for their clients, should the agencies they were dealing with 'join up', was not something they necessarily saw as important in those days, the Scottish initiatives being something of an exception in the British context. Instead, what they developed in their communities, usually over time, was a strong focus, a sense of commitment and a willingness to bridge agency divides by reaching out to anyone who could assist, whether these individuals were based in a statutory agency or, as was frequently the case, not. They appreciated the absolute necessity of becoming well informed, through research and detailed case work, of the nature of their client group and what all agencies statutory and non-statutory could offer. Through this process they became familiar with what could be expected of their colleagues in other agencies, and of any gaps in provision, within a fairly well defined locality.

Sometimes this led to unexpected outcomes. For example, one such group, in the 1980s, investigating the support required for adult, mentally disturbed, homeless petty offenders found that their original hypothesis was, on closer investigation, very wide of the mark. They had thought initially that lack of accommodation was the problem, leading them to think about raising money for a purpose-built hostel. Their research showed them that, on the contrary, there was plenty of accommodation but the proprietors who could provide it needed to be sure, before offering their services, that they could call on immediate back-up should they feel concerned about the behaviour of their very vulnerable lodgers. This led to the development of a multiprofessional community support team working at the interface between a wide range of agencies (Roaf 2002). We see the same pattern in schools, where teachers can be convinced of their ability to teach young people with significant physical or behavioural difficulties when they are assured of the availability of assistance and advice from a support team.

The early multiprofessional workers tended to be reflective practitioners and lateral thinkers. This habit of mind, grounded in case work, which by its nature took them to the margins of each agency, led them to consider a range of long-term preventative solutions which were often innovative and inexpensive. Members of one multiprofessional team working with young people on the margins in the 1990s reported that 'by accessing the work of other agencies the range of programmes [they could offer] was improved ... the initiative provided spin offs and creative thinking ... it developed its own momentum so that after a while [the team] was thinking more creatively' (Roaf 2002: 76). The significant point here is that the inspiration for innovation came, not from the centre of agencies, but from individual practitioners working with socially excluded individuals at the margins.

Social exclusion

Over and above questions on how agencies are configured, and in spite of many successes, new threats to children and young people emerge all the time. These may arise from the discovery of new disabling conditions or more especially from, for example, the environment, migration or poverty, and they require political will of a different order to address. The risk factors known to lead to the possibility of social exclusion have long been familiar. An OECD survey (1995) across a range of countries and cultures identified seven groups of predictive (and predictable) risk factors: poverty and social class; ethnic minority status; family issues; poor knowledge of the majority language; type of school; geography; and community factors. From their reports of the different countries involved the OECD produced a definition which saw children and young people at risk as 'those who were failing at school and who are unsuccessful in making the transition to work and adult life and as a consequence are unlikely to make a full contribution to the active society' (OECD 1995: 21, 47).

Likewise, the multiplying effects of risk factors have been known for a long time. Rutter's 1980 study suggested that although with one risk factor the likelihood of serious consequences occurred with the same probability as no risk factors, two or three risk factors increased the chances of serious consequences four-fold, and with four the risk was increased ten-fold. Practical experience suggests that these probabilities still apply. More recently, UNICEF's (2007) report on child well-being in rich countries provides damning evidence of the very poor performance of the UK across five of the six dimensions used in this study. With one-third (up from 10 per cent in 1979) of all children in the UK living in poverty (End Child Poverty, 2007) and targets to halve this proportion by 2010 unlikely to be met, it is clear that there are major underlying issues beyond the scope of children's services to address, however reconfigured. Much can indeed be achieved by improved coordination between front line services for children and families and with a sharper focus on the interfaces between agencies. But unless these underlying issues concerning the quality of universal provision, and the disempowerment and discrimination particularly associated with poverty, are satisfactorily addressed, the benefits of improved multiprofessional working are unlikely to be realized and could, at best, be regarded as papering over the cracks. We need to look further afield for some clues as to how the whole system can be designed to work more effectively to improve the lives of children and young people.

Learning from development studies

The idea that the well-being of children and young people is a matter for the whole system (often expressed in the cliché, 'It takes a whole village to raise a child') has informed many aspects of government policy in recent years, in relation to children's services both in the UK and elsewhere. Whatever the much disputed provenance of the aphorism, its association with development studies is relevant. In the early 1980s, professional concern about marginalized communities and their young people coincided, in education circles at least, with a major interest in human rights and development education, generated by a sequence of human rights legislation (e.g. the Sex Discrimination Act 1975; the Race Discrimination Act 1976; up to and beyond the 1989 Children Act with its then radical requirement that children should be consulted and listened to in matters which affect them (section 17). In such a climate, those working with socially excluded young people, in and out of school (the latter including teachers of English as a Second Language, community educators, youth workers and social workers), found a common cause. With a growing gap between rich and poor in the UK it was not uncommon at development education conferences in the late 1980s to hear the term 'third world' applied to some parts of Britain.

Clearly there were parallels and lessons to be learnt at home from non-governmental organizations working with excluded groups abroad. 'Working together' became an important, if at that time peripheral, activity taking place in lunch breaks and outside normal working hours. Discussion in these meetings tended to focus on the issues arising out of their case work, between practitioners who recognized that they needed the support of colleagues outside their own agency to work effectively with socially excluded young people. From the near tragedy-level of some of the case work, surely, these practitioners thought, there was some longer-term solution to prevent such situations arising again?

In considering this question, the metaphor used by aid agencies to describe the relationship between targeted and universal responses to injustice is helpful at several levels. It tells a story, which can be adapted to suit local circumstances, of women living in a riverside community whose menfolk have been taken away to fight or work elsewhere. After weeks of waiting with no news, the women begin to notice people floating downstream. Some they save, others are already dead. To prevent further tragedy they decide to go upstream. The metaphor of the river is important, first, because it is clear that upstream and downstream are part of the same river. Responses to injustice, whether immediate or long-term, reactive or proactive, are all part of the same system. Second, appropriate action is based on careful observation and analysis. Those found in extremis are examined, not only to preserve life and life chances but for what their plight can contribute to an understanding of causes and the changes needed upstream. Third, the metaphor emphasizes the part relatively powerless people can play in improving the whole system by their ability to observe, cooperate and act. Taking this a step further, one can speculate as to what the outcome might have been, had the power relations in that riverside community been different, and had there been better communication and more equitable participation in decision making between different groups.

Sen's (1999) analysis of development in his book *Democracy as Freedom* affirms the fundamental importance of the freedoms of individuals, particularly

> to the expansion of the 'capabilities' of persons to lead the kind of lives they value – and have reason to value. These capabilities can be enhanced by public policy, but also, on the other side, the direction of public policy can be influenced by the effective use of participatory capabilities of the public. The *two-way relationship* is central ...
>
> (p. 18, original emphasis)

Sen explains why individual freedom is so important in the concept of development. In his analysis, freedom is central to the process of development, since it encourages people to help themselves and to influence the world – to become agents in bringing about change, becoming active as members of the public, able to participate in economic, social and political activity. He stresses that this is much more than a simple question of income, but rather of capability – the capability an individual has to lead the kind of life he or she values and has reason to value. Clearly poverty is an important factor leading to loss of agency, with regard, for example, to health, education and employment. But even more important, according to Sen, is the capability that comes from the democratic right to have one's voice heard and to have that voice treated with equality and respect. In this book our intention is to demonstrate that a key role for multiprofessional activity is to build the relationships which will enhance the capabilities of children and young people, as they are in the here and now, not simply their future capabilities, and to allow the direction of public policy to be influenced by their participation. This implies that the system or systems responsible for the well-being of children and their families should also enhance the agency of parents, carers and the practitioners who work most closely with children and young people.

The policy framework

In response to this kind of analysis, *Every Child Matters: Change for Children* (DfES 2004) demonstrates, for the first time, a thorough-going commitment to providing a joined up policy context for multiagency initiatives. The expression of the five outcomes to be secured through *Every Child Matters*, shaped by children themselves (be healthy; stay safe; enjoy and achieve; make a positive contribution; achieve economic well-being), can be seen as a genuine attempt to enhance capability in Sen's (1999) sense of the capability of individuals not only to lead the kind of life 'they value, and have reason to value', but also, crucially, to participate in directing public policy.

The *Every Child Matters* agenda, framed in response to children's concerns, also underlines the impossibility of achieving these outcomes without a response from the whole community. And it is this response which the agencies must strive, and indeed are now striving, to promote through mutual cooperation. Scotland's Integrated Community Schools (ICS) programme, committed to addressing social inclusion, lifelong learning and active citizenship, was initiated some years earlier in 1998 with 'the goal of delivering public services that meet the needs of its citizens – parents, pupils and communities – rather than the convenience of public service providers' (Tett 2005: 160).

ICS provides some good examples of how national policy works out in practice. In many cases these are seemingly simple and straightforward practical tasks, such as setting up a 'drop in for coffee' session (Illsley and Redford 2005), designed to engage the wider community and gradually expanding into something much more influential.

> The ordinary nuts and bolts holding together the inter-agency for inclusion engine are taxis, childcare, finance, coffee and ... room. The evidence points to how space plays a role: having spaces where the different agencies can meet and interact both formally and informally allows for various levels of voluntary engagement. The surface-level pragmatic activity may hide more significant shifts when inclusive inter-agency working is afoot.
> (Glenny and Mannion 2005: 155)

In these settings, young people, parents and members of the community are able, through the growth of trusting relationships, to begin to see themselves as having agency in Sen's (1999) sense, able to contribute positively to the school and its community and to realize their own potential. That this is so, is demonstrated by the unprecedented number (19,000) of responses received from young people to the consultation exercise on the Green Paper *Youth Matters* (DfES 2005) and their influence on its outcome: *Youth Matters: Next Steps* (DfES 2006a).

Developing multiprofessional communication systems

As part of its commitment to the provision of a joined up policy context for multiprofessional working, *Every Child Matters* provides guidance for the development of services, incorporating, for example, a *Common Assessment Framework* and the notion of the *Lead Professional*. However, it stops short of providing blueprints for action. In so doing it creates the possibility for building on experience and practice at a local level. This leaves local managers with the responsibility for developing their services to meet a complex new agenda. And in doing this they can draw on a wealth of advice. For example, the NFER review *Effective Interagency Working* (Tomlinson 2003), building on the findings of earlier studies, lists the following factors that underline effective partnerships:

- full strategic and operational commitment to collaboration;
- an awareness of agencies' differing aims and values, with a commitment to working towards a common goal;
- involvement of relevant people, often including clients and their carers;
- clear roles and responsibilities for individuals and agencies involved in collaboration;
- supportive and committed management of staff in partnerships;
- flexible and innovative funding mechanisms;
- systems for interagency collecting, sharing and analysis of data;
- joint training, with accreditation where appropriate;
- strategies to encourage team commitment beyond the personal interests of key individuals;
- effective and appropriate communication between agencies and professionals;
- a suitable, and sometimes altered, location for the delivery of services.

How can local managers make use of such advice? How can they arrive at similarly effective partnerships? Implementing the kind of agenda implied in the above list is undeniably complex. Now, this is not in any way to suggest that the list has no value: it has been distilled from evaluations of a number of multiagency initiatives, and identifies the factors that impact positively and negatively on partnership. Indeed the factors identified concur with the findings of our own research. However, in the examples we saw, most of these factors had never been set up as initial objectives, rather they had emerged as a function of effective projects, as a result of the creation of good multiagency environments developed over a number of years. By contrast, when we observed local authority managers restructuring to meet the multiagency agenda, it seemed that considerable amounts of time were spent in consultations with groups of managers from the various agencies. At these meetings complex diagrams were drawn to represent line management maps and, at the end of the day, the final highly negotiated result was seen by the people on the ground who deliver the services, as something imposed upon them. Frustrated by the whole process, having felt in limbo for the year or so that the restructuring had taken, many of them failed to engage with enthusiasm. In the health services this restructuring had become an annual event. The problem with a list such as the one above, is that it suggests the setting up of new structures and processes without recognizing that the restructuring process in itself seems to be disruptive to existing good multiprofessional practices.

So we have a paradox, implementing change towards facilitating interagency development can be, in itself, disruptive to those processes. Other, less disruptive, approaches to achieving the desired objectives need to be found. Part of the problem is the question of timescales. Effective projects have tended to evolve over time as trust between partners developed and the purposes for which the project was set up become clear. Managers looking at researchers' lists of factors are apt to forget that these lists are compiled from a range of projects each one of which took place over a number of years and none of which was likely to display all the factors identified by the review as contributing to success. It is tempting therefore to examine the list and make a start on it in a top-down and piecemeal fashion, perhaps on a scheme to collect, share and analyse data or to develop some joint training initiatives or a directory of local resources. Most areas will not in any case be starting from scratch and there will be areas of good practice to build on.

In this book our analysis suggests that the existence of an effective communication system is the key factor underpinning everything and from which other aspects of successful practice follow. In particular we are interested in the extent to which local communication systems encourage or inhibit the free flow of information and feedback and the extent to which children and young people, their families and carers and the practitioners who work most closely with them are included in this system. The following list, quoted by Mott (2004: 10), is typical of many others enumerating barriers to effective multiprofessional working:

- the large number of agencies, disciplines and services involved;
- each agency having different perspectives, expertise, priorities, geographical boundaries, management structures, training arrangements, working practices, legislative frameworks and monitoring arrangements;
- lack of opportunity for shared training;
- professional protectiveness, insecurity and fear of losing control;
- traditional practice, reluctance to work in a different way and fear of changes;
- feelings of superiority;
- lack of knowledge of the roles and responsibilities of others;
- lack of awareness of the benefits of working together;
- differing expectations from within own agency and other services.

Our studies suggest that most of these barriers can be addressed when practitioners in a local community have the opportunity through a local forum to meet together regularly over a number of years (in our experience at least three) to share the issues arising out of their practice over time. Both the size of the geographical area and the length of time required for trust to develop and action to follow are critical. Successful multiprofessional working develops, in geographical terms, in relatively small areas over long timescales. This long-term time frame, allowing for the emergence of local responses to pressing issues and the resolution of controversy, plays a crucial role in building resilient communities. The management change required in local authorities and national government is to support and nurture such initiatives: to foster their development without imposing uniformity and to promote the dissemination of good practice as it emerges. The significance of local forums for the discussion of agency and interagency issues is that it appears to supply the element missing from wider agency and multiprofessional communication systems operating in local and national government. Yet without this element, senior managers and policy makers are deprived of the essential feedback from the margins they need to shape services to enhance the capabilities of the individuals they so clearly want to benefit.

Meeting the challenges of multiprofessional working: avoiding collaborative inertia

In spite of the difficulties experienced by those putting interagency policy into effect, there is no question but that the requirement to think professionally in terms of interagency activity has been a great advance: a vindication of the work of professionals going back a long way to, for example, the Kilbrandon Report (1964) and the child guidance centres of the 1960s (Sampson 1980). It has indeed been a step forward to bring agencies and professionals together, but to achieve the outcomes expected of it, policy makers promoting interagency collaboration must now recognize that the engine of good practice lies in close attention to the evidence of practitioners working at or beyond agency boundaries, 'eager to cross borders in order to gain different perspectives' (Moss and Petrie 2002: 166).

Recent research is encouraging in its interest in probing challenging aspects of multiprofessional working, much needed if the threat of 'collaborative inertia' raised by Huxham and Vangen (2005) is to be avoided. This need is made both more significant and more challenging in the context of the rapid expansion of extended schools and children's centres. Warin's (2007) research, for example, investigates the problems caused by the tensions which can occur when field workers find themselves trying to serve the interest of children and families simultaneously. In a different field, concerning the underlying and sometimes conflicting values of those involved in multiprofessional activity, Tett (2000) teases out the very different approaches that can be adopted by schools in their work with students regarded as at risk of exclusion. There is much too to be learnt from other countries with different cultures and value systems. Petrie et al. (in press) draw on a comparison of Swedish and English multiprofessional practice to raise a number of important issues for the UK to address – significant, since both countries are undergoing similar changes and show a similar commitment to multiprofessional working. Turning to the question of evaluation, Tanner et al. (2006: 4) discuss the question of what 'quality' means in early years services. 'Central to this debate has been the extent to which quality is understood as objective and static or subjective and dynamic', an issue which will find common cause among all those involved in the evaluation of multiprofessional initiatives. These are examples only of a welcome and widening debate to which we hope this book will contribute.

The research base

The purpose of this book is to reflect on research studies of effective multiprofessional practice and to examine what underlying processes are at work in the development of the effective communication systems on which such practice relies. The research presented draws on a series of small case studies, collected over a seven-year period. The case studies describe and discuss the services around six different school clusters, typically a large secondary school, feeder primaries and local children's centres, ranging from high-need urban areas to medium- to low-need county towns with their satellite villages. Two of the cluster studies were reviewed three times over the seven-year period providing an opportunity to examine their development over time (Glenny 2000, 2001, 2005a, b). In the latest study, all six clusters were reviewed together (Glenny 2005a) allowing some of the findings from the earlier studies to be used as a framework for looking at the wider sample.

In each cluster area, representatives from schools and support services were interviewed and selected case studies of individual children and collaborative projects were reviewed. The systems of communication and resulting patterns of action that had developed around each cluster of schools were mapped using 'rich pictures' (Checkland and Scholes 1999). The cluster areas were selected because they were experimenting with new ways of developing 'joined up working', in some cases through local initiatives, in some through local authority encouragement and in others through both. They were therefore not typical examples of practice across the authority.

In addition to the cluster studies, data have also been drawn from evaluations of three projects where joint working was an essential component. Two of these were supported by the local children's fund, one focusing on the role of the *home school community link worker* (Glenny 2007a) and the other on a *service* targeting young people from ages 8 to 13 in danger of entering the criminal justice system (Glenny 2007b). The third explored the relationship between educational psychologists and speech and language therapists in the identification and support of children with language difficulties (Glenny and Lown 1987). In each evaluation, detailed case studies of individual children were reviewed, drawing on interviews with field workers, members of the schools and support services with whom they worked and the parents, carers and children for whom the services were designed.

In reviewing the findings from these evaluations, we have been concerned to identify the ways in which individuals make sense of their experience of working together, drawing on *personal construct psychology* (Kelly 1955). However, we were struck by the way in which the context created by the multiple interactions of field workers influenced both the way individuals 'constructed' their experience and their possibilities for action. To explore this we have adopted a variety of approaches to systemic analysis. Key influences have been the work of Vickers ([1965] 1995), whose thinking was to make an important contribution to the work of Checkland and Scholes (1999) on *soft systems methodology*, and Stacey's work (2001) on the analysis of *complex responsive processes* in organizations. At the same time, while most of the documented research on multiprofessional practice among those working with children has focused on the work of relatively tightly bounded teams, we were observing a much looser and more informal type of collaborative activity. For this reason, in order to draw out explanatory themes from the data, we have compared our findings with examples of collaborative endeavour in contexts other than that of children's services.

Overview

Chapter 2 outlines the research base, namely an analysis of a series of case studies in terms of 'what works and why' in multiprofessional communication systems. In Chapter 3 these data are drawn on to consider how communication systems evolved and contributed to success in two of the cases studied. These findings are compared with other research exploring multiprofessional partnerships to draw out the common principles underlying effective communication systems. The chapter introduces Vicker's ([1965] 1995) concept of an 'appreciative system' and proposes the development of a new role, that of 'system minder', which these case studies indicate has a central, but so far insufficiently regarded, role to play in the development of an effective communication system in a field dominated by complexity. Chapter 4 discusses the relatively new, but rapidly developing, role of the home school community link worker. This role is significant in providing an example of the way in which an appreciative system allows support services to customize their provision to meet local needs. Chapter 5 provides a discussion of the dilemmas and constraints that determine the characteristic configuration and dynamics of a particular system. The focus here is on the observation emerging from the case studies, that 'successful' multiprofessional forums specifically address 'upstream and downstream' provision not as separate entities but as coherent aspects of the same dynamic system: seeing, in other words, upstream and downstream, as described earlier in this Introduction, as part of the same metaphorical river. This central notion is explored further in terms of four key questions:

1   What is the appropriate balance between upstream and down-stream work?
2   How is the transition between universal and specialist services managed?
3   To what extent should resources be shared between working with children and working with their families?
4   How can service users be enabled to shape local services?

Chapter 6, building on insights gained in Chapters 4 and 5 concerning the role of the link worker and the system minder, considers the importance of relationships in the field, exploring such issues as underlying differences in values and purposes; different approaches to common tasks; the perspectives of service users; conflicting constructions of childhood; trust; the different mechanisms for regulation and measurement; and the question of risk and responsibility.

The book concludes its discussion of 'what works and why' with a consideration of 'the structure of magic': what it is that underpins successful practice despite the many different means by which such success has been achieved. The authors conclude that the study of the dynamics of complexity offers an illuminative theoretical framework for studying such multiprofessional communication systems.

2 The research base: exploring multiprofessional communication systems in action

As a school governor of a primary school, one of us (Glenny) had become increasingly concerned by the amount of time the head teacher of the school was spending trying to sort out concerns about children at risk from emotional and physical neglect and ill treatment. The head teacher was not the named person for child protection (this role belonged to the special educational needs (SEN) coordinator) but the head became involved because the children did not appear to meet social services thresholds. Therefore, since no help outside the school was available, the problems were bounced back to the school to deal with.

The head teacher and her colleagues had to manage the issues using their very limited flexible resources, that is, the class teacher's time after classes had finished, normally allocated to preparing for the next day's teaching; the SEN coordinator's time, only employed for two days a week, time normally allocated to working with children who needed additional support with their learning; or the head's time, normally allocated to running a school to achieve the best possible educational outcomes for the 350 children in her care.

The level of need identified by the school staff was a constant concern to them. On a daily basis they had to watch children's lives unravelling, taking what could be years before other agencies regarded the issues as serious enough to intervene. On a daily basis, teachers had the dilemma of splitting their time between one needy child and the rest of their class, containing a number of only slightly less needy children. On a daily basis they were faced with the question of what is a 'good enough' teacher. These anxieties were further amplified by their lack of knowledge about the right way to tackle those concerns. Perhaps they were worrying too much, perhaps they were not communicating the right information to alert social services, perhaps there was something else they should be doing? These concerns, linked to the fact that doing anything would leave them no time to prepare for the next day, generated a high level of impotent and exhausting anxiety.

The school had two dilemmas. What to do with:

1 the children who genuinely fell below the social services thresholds, for example, the children with levels of physical and emotional neglect that had a clear impact on their attendance, their ability to function in school and indeed their general well-being, but which were not intense enough to warrant additional support;
2 those who were at the threshold of requiring social services intervention, but for which the school couldn't provide the right kinds of evidence to engage the attention of a very busy social work team, struggling with staffing shortages.

These observations triggered the research outlined here (Glenny 2001). To check the school's judgement on this latter category, evidence was collected on the six case studies causing the school most concern and these were taken to the local social services manager. She agreed they were all cases meeting threshold criteria that should have been followed up by social services following referral.

So the system was not working in a number of ways: schools did not have the time and/or the experience necessary for the detailed case work to act as advocate for their most vulnerable children; important decisions about children were being made in 'marginal' time, time when competing pressures truncated the length and quality of discussion that took place; the anxiety this caused was further exacerbated by the fact that there is no provision for supervision in school and so no expectation that emotional wear and tear be shared and supported outside the informal friendship networks operating in schools.

Meanwhile the social services team was so stretched and thresholds were so high, that children could not receive support until their needs had become very great, and in all probability their problems too entrenched to be easily remedied. At the same time social workers did not have the spare capacity to engage with colleagues in schools in talking through cases and so were not able to help them in supporting the children who had not yet reached threshold level, developing case work skills or making effective referrals.

The picture then was one of a failure of the school and social services to mesh effectively, to the extent that children's life chances were endangered. Even more seriously, the levels of stress resulting for all concerned meant that no one had any spare capacity to do anything about the situation: it was just an unfortunate feature of everybody's working context, which nobody felt they had the power to remedy.

Conversations with head teachers in neighbouring schools revealed that this communication failure between schools and social services was a common experience, and that it did not just apply to social services but to many aspects of the multidisciplinary support that schools received. As a result of these discussions the head teachers commissioned a survey of the experience of the cluster of schools with all their support services. This is described below as study 1.

Study 1: baseline study

The children and families in the locality studied represent a vulnerable group from an urban estate with high indices for economic disadvantage, alcohol and drug use and single parent families. The six schools in the sample (an upper school and feeder middle and first schools) are experienced at working with children with a variety of special needs and have used their additional funding in a range of ways to support the high incidence of children with special educational need in their community. Our study involved interviewing key personnel within schools, and field workers and managers in the support services working with those schools, and collecting individual case studies of children to see how the system of support impacted upon their experiences.

The system doesn't work!

The findings from this study were uniformly bleak. Nobody interviewed was happy with what was happening. A key feature of the interview data was a frequent reference to 'the system', for example interviewees talked of the 'school system', the 'system of support', the 'resourcing system', 'dysfunction of the system', 'inflexibility of the system', being 'let down by the system'. There were regular reports that 'the system doesn't work': indeed there were no examples in the interview data of a sense of human agency that could bring change. In tracking down possible causes for this, the experience of individual children was followed through to explore any common patterns that emerged. The following case examples are anonymized and simplified but representative in terms of level and complexity of need of the individual scenarios schools needed to resolve.

Tom and Joe

A new family arrive half way through the autumn term following a family move from another county. Tom is 8 and his brother Joe is 6 years old. It soon becomes clear that Tom's behaviour is very disruptive and periodically violent and his educational attainment is very low. The receiving school have expertise in working with challenging children but are finding him difficult to manage. His papers are slow to arrive from the previous school and a waiting list for the educational psychologist means that he can't be seen straight away. Working with the behaviour support team the school adopts a temporary containment strategy to try to minimize the disruption caused to other children. They are also concerned about younger brother Joe's very low levels of attainment and his lack of response to a reading programme they have put in place for him. Eventually, the brothers' previous school files arrive, and although patchy and incomplete, Tom's indicates that he was close to permanent exclusion having been at the school for only two terms following transfer from another school in the same area. Joe's file shows evidence of concern for what seems to be serious developmental delay, but he had moved before appointments with specialists had been followed through. Both files also indicated child protection concerns and so social services are informed. The psychologist's report, achieved by the end of the autumn term, suggests that both brothers have levels of need that require additional resources and possible special school placement, and multiprofessional assessments are set up. This process takes until Easter to progress to the point where extra resources are available to the school – well within acceptable timescales for the 'statementing' procedure, but the process has still left the school without any additional resources for a seven-month period.

This case study illustrates a number of themes that were common in the overall data collected. First, in terms of communication:

- Information is lost in the transition between schools: there is no responsibility for 'handover' between schools, even though children who frequently move settings are known to be particularly vulnerable;
- A number of professionals were drawn into this case but without strategic or coordinated direction in the initial stages, making the process of gaining statutory assessment and, indeed, developing good quality conversations about the children, difficult and time consuming.

Second, the protocols around the allocation of resources build inflexibility into the system of support:

- There is a high incidence of crisis management for situations that recur regularly, created by a lack of flexibility around the resources available in the early stages of the response.

- Young people in need are often in assessment limbo for considerable periods of time.
- Protocols for allocating resources on the basis of relative need result in considerable amounts of field work time going into 'making a case' that is watertight enough for panel members who don't know the case, to make a decision about it; the costs of running these panels are very expensive: in relation to a statement of special educational need, the Audit Commission (2002) estimates that on average this costs £4000 per child.
- The assessment process uses up disproportionate amounts of the available resource time, leaving support personnel little remaining resource for therapeutic intervention.
- Children and families perceived as having problems may be drawing in a number of agencies, but only receiving small amounts of uncoordinated help from these multiple sources; conversely, the focus on structuring services around individual interventions creates a mismatch between what is available and what is needed at any given time.

This again was a feature of many of the case studies, illustrated in the following example.

Daniel

Daniel is a 9-year-old boy with receptive language difficulties. He finds it difficult to concentrate and has poor basic levels of attainment. He is disruptive and deeply frustrated by his communication difficulties. He lives with his younger sister and his mother who is depressed and finds his behaviour at home increasingly unmanageable. His speech and language therapy has been withdrawn because of poor attendance for appointments due to his mother being unable to organize transport and/ or childcare. His first term at middle school is heading for breakdown because of his frequent absences and disruptive behaviour. Although his mother would appreciate support and this is seen to be a key element in Daniel's situation, she does not meet the threshold requirements to ensure social services involvement and there are no other resources available for this option. Daniel has also been assessed for attendance at the local language centre but there are no places free there at the moment. As a result Daniel is placed at a weekly residential school for children with moderate learning difficulties and emotional and behavioural problems. Daniel is unhappy about this because he doesn't want to leave home and enjoys playing football with his friends at his old school.

This placement will cost £25,000 as opposed to the £1425 of a mainstream placement or the £3500 at a language centre. In educational terms it will offer smaller classes and ensure access to regular speech and language support. However, the transition is difficult for Daniel because nobody in the new school understands his speech and the football is at such a low standard that he does not enjoy playing football there.

Thus inflexibilities in the structuring of services mean that:

- The individual focus of the assessment process restricts the discussion of structural issues affecting a number of young people – in this example, other children at Daniel's school were missing speech therapy because parents were unable to get them to their appointments at the clinic.
- Children were being offered less ideal solutions that were more expensive than preferred solutions, because the latter were unavailable; in this example, support for the mother and access to speech therapy at school would have been a much cheaper option than any of the special placements being offered.
- Threshold gateways to professional help mean intervention is often provided too late, when the child's/family's circumstances have deteriorated to a point where they are not easily improved; in this example, Daniel had slipped through the net of appropriate provision because his mother had not been able to get him to the specialist support that would have triggered an earlier response to his language problems.
- Children's own choices are often lost in the process of getting the 'right placement'.

Systemic failure

These case studies illustrate the complex and interconnected nature of the problems of organizing support for vulnerable children and young people. They also demonstrate why individual field workers feel so helpless and that their hands are tied by 'the system'. The examples demonstrate how the organization of relationships and resources to support children's well-being and inclusion in school can operate to produce poor value for money and counter-productive outcomes.

It could be argued that more successful case studies could have been selected, but the pattern of data overall suggested that there were clear systemic failures in the organization of the services that required systemic solutions. These systemic failures are due not to the failure of particular school staff members or field workers, rather to features of the organizational structures in which they are embedded. Thus the organization of support was problematic in a number of ways with the identified areas of dysfunction both interlinked and apparently intractable. Most significantly there seemed to be no self-correcting mechanisms: problems were recognized but they were impossible for any one person or agency, acting alone, to overcome. To explore this further, it was important to represent the communication systems operating around this group of schools. Tools for system analysis developed by Checkland and Scholes (1999) were adopted and the relationships in this particular communication system were drawn using a 'rich picture' shown as Figure 2.1.

Figure 2.1 illustrates why school personnel were feeling so frustrated and the issues seemed so irresolvable. The stacked circles in the diagram represent the different schools, and the diagram shows the lines of communication for the first school in the stack. As the pattern of communication was very similar for all schools, a multiplication of the lines of communication by the number of schools would give a representation of the whole system in the local area studied. Figure 2.1

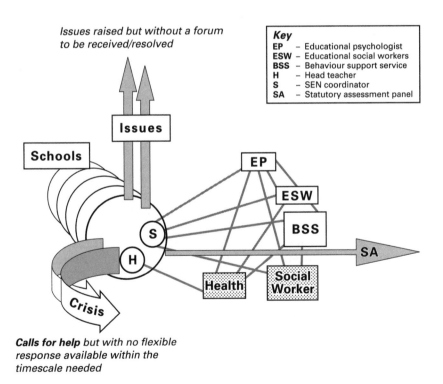

Figure 2.1 Communication systems: baseline study

shows the number of communication links that everyone is having to service. Examining this communication system, alongside the data from respondents, it became clear that a number of these links were not operating well.

First, the issues raised and expressed by individual head teachers were not being heard by anybody who could do anything about them. At different times, different head teachers had expressed concerns but hadn't been able to resolve the issues. Their concerns would be expressed to the various apparently relevant local authority managers (although it was often not clear who the most relevant contact might be), and in due course a lengthy and courteous letter would be received from a local authority officer, explaining how nothing could be done. A number of heads were able to show us such letters sent in response to letters they or their chair of governors had sent. What was interesting was the similarity of the letters sent from the different head teachers. The issues were the same across the different schools and the discourse largely focused on the need for additional resources and the current lack of them. Field workers also had common concerns but there was no forum for reaching consensus or a resolution. Equally, the issues raised were not being received in any systematic way.

Second, the plethora of support services available (simplified in Figure 2.1) required a large number of communication links for head teachers and special educational needs (SEN) coordinators to service in order to achieve help. Further, at any given time most of these people were away from their office on case work and so were not easily contactable. Consequently, each of the links in the diagram had to be repeatedly travelled before contact was made, a process taking very significant proportions of SEN coordinators' time.

Third, at times of crisis, the already overstretched support services could rarely provide the speedy response necessary to provide school personnel with the support they needed. Schools, having invested time in seeking help, often did not receive it and were left to deal with these situations alone (represented in the Figure 2.1 diagram as the crisis arrow, bouncing concerns back to the school). School personnel, not surprisingly, experienced considerable stress because they felt both out of their depth and under time pressure. As a result they would take their concerns about particular children to the first field worker available even if he or she was not really the right person. This caused the support service personnel to feel they were often being put under pressure and being used inappropriately by schools. This had led them therefore to develop various ways of keeping what they felt to be 'insatiable demands', at bay, so that they could protect their time to do 'at least something properly'.

Achieving change

The communication channels represented in Figure 2.1 illustrate the difficulties facing an individual trying to achieve action for change within such a complex net of relationships. For example, if an individual support worker unilaterally decides to prioritize early interventions, they will quickly find themselves with an impossible case load and will be seen not to be meeting their statutory duties. If a service decides to shift its operations from individual case work to a consultancy-based approach – for example, helping schools with issues that affect groups of children, and developing in-school skills, practices and policies that will ultimately support them in being more inclusive – the time available for detailed case work on complex cases then disappears. Meanwhile the need for resolution of complex cases just creates pressure in another part of the system for schools and other case workers. Thus, even if the innovation is perceived to be successful by some members of 'the system', the knock-on effects can be problematic for others who may not be involved and/or have no understanding of the reasons for the original decision.

It can also be seen here that small systems, for example individual service practices, are embedded within larger systems – looking, in this case, at the range of people involved with children and young people in a particular area – and need to be operating in relation to the larger systems. In the baseline study this coherence was absent and in particular there was no way of discussing the deployment of field workers in terms of the optimum times for interventions. Preventative approaches and reactive approaches were happening independently of each other, a function of different funding streams and historical service provision, rather than any systematic analysis of community need.

Roaf (2002) has applied the terms 'upstream' and 'downstream' to the monitoring of the timing of interventions and to the connection that exists between long- and short-term responses to problems. The analogy of taking a walk upstream to see why we are finding people floating in the river downstream is helpful in drawing attention to the continuity of experience and the role of context in the definition of need.

Representing the data in terms of the 'upstream–downstream' analogy, it became clear why schools were so stressed by their responsibilities for children. Schools, as the universally used service, were likely to be the first to recognize concerns about young children and their families, and this placed a particularly heavy responsibility upon them to sustain the communication links. For other services, the children were invisible if no attention was drawn to them, unlike for schools where their daily presence or absence was visible and pressing. In the locality studied, schools very often picked up concerns about these children years before the children met the thresholds necessary to justify interventions. They were helplessly watching these children in the river with no clear means of rescue. For this reason when they did manage to engage the interest of other services, they were anxious to offload the responsibility for the children as quickly as possible so that they could attend to other children further up the river. For the other services, with no sense of this history, this was often perceived as ruthless and uncooperative. At the point where the other agencies, fresh to the case, were seeking to work collaboratively with schools, the relationship between the child and the school had been pushed to the limit, following years of effort, and as a result had often irretrievably broken down.

There are never enough resources!

Another feature of the interview data collected was that it was dominated by a discourse about resources. Head teachers and governors often wrote in terms of a need for more resources, and local authority officers would they write back, politely pointing out that there were no more resources. However, the data suggested that a lot of the resources were being wasted because of the communication difficulties everyone was experiencing. The expense of 'making the case' for panel procedures has already been noted (pp. 18–19), and evidence from the Audit Commission report (2002) makes it clear that the informal professional conversations and advice given by psychologists to SEN coordinators on first investigation of a case was the contribution they appreciated most and this was rarely improved upon by the lengthy process of making it into a case for the local authority panel. Similarly the SEN coordinators interviewed in this study were routinely spending the majority of their time in preparing paperwork for the panel or phoning field workers to coordinate their contributions to panel processes. And this was a tension for them because this was time they felt they should have been spending on learning support activities. These included, for example, working with children who needed support with literacy or study skills or anger management programmes and supporting other colleagues in developing teaching strategies and materials: ironically, all being activities that they were seeking the extra resources to carry out.

The finding that the children and families in the case studies were receiving small amounts of help from many different groups of professionals was another example of resources being wasted. Costed out, these short-term interventions and multiple assessments cost the equivalent amount of one professional providing a significant and sustained level of support for the same child and their family. However, in order for this preferable situation to be secured, effective communication needed to take place. Overall, it was clear from this study that the available resources were not being used optimally.

Study 2: the urban context

Study 2 was based on an initiative developed as a direct response to the concerns raised by study 1, and focused on the same group of schools that were involved in the previous study with the addition of the other half of the partnership. As a result, interviews were held with many of the same people who contributed to the original study. The partnership consisted of 15 schools, one secondary, two special, three middle and nine first schools. The study was carried out one year after the introduction of the initiative, and 18 months after study 1 was completed. The data from the first study was therefore used as a baseline for comparison with the data from this study.

Receiving and resolving the issues

The initiative entitled Integrated Support Services (ISS) was designed as a strand of an education action zone (EAZ) bid, which meant it was supported by a clear project management structure and a small independent resource budget. To achieve the aims of the ISS initiative, a steering group was set up, namely the ISS core group. This group was chaired by the ISS coordinator and included representatives from schools, pupil support services, LEA officers and advisers, voluntary agencies and, in its later stages, social and health care and the primary health care trust. The initial function of the group was to respond to the primary concern raised in the baseline study, which was to provide a place where issues and concerns could be received and an audit begun of the needs of vulnerable children, young people and their families in the local area served by the school partnership. The implications for the communication system can be seen in Figure 2.2. The core group receives information from the schools, their support services and other agencies, and is tasked with discussing and resolving the issues and feeding back their actions.

The ISS core group had members from different levels of the organizations represented and this produced a particular richness of dialogue and allowed direct feedback from a range of positions and perspectives. Thus, although initiated by the EAZ bidding process, the project was rooted within the locality drawing strongly on the

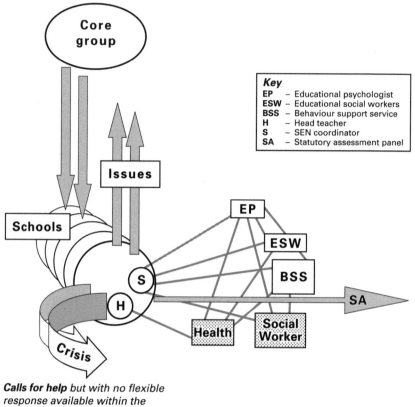

Calls for help but with no flexible
response available within the
timescale needed

Figure 2.2 The urban context: stage 1

experience of local schools and field workers. The ISS coordinator was a part time (0.5) appointment drawn from the group of local practitioners already working in the partnership, and funded by the EAZ. The coordinator was effectively the project manager for the ISS.

Typically, the group focused on identifying issues regarding access to, and/or gaps in, provision. Responses included information-finding exercises, reviewing protocols and setting up pilot projects to meet identified needs. Strategies proposed by the group were further discussed and agreed on by the LEA heads of service group and the partnership head teacher forum. Thus these key bodies were tied together with feedback loops that ensured all parties were involved and informed.

Following their initial audit of need, the ISS core group sought to address one of the key problems identified in study 1: how to rationalize

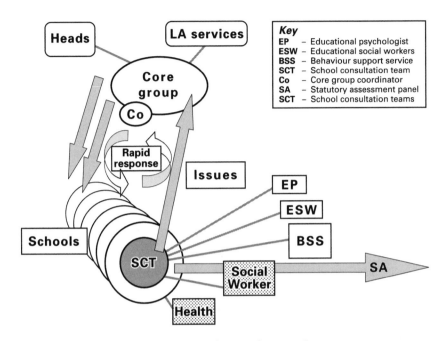

Figure 2.3 Communication system: urban study, stage 2

the communication between schools and personnel from the different services and agencies so that communication would be less time consuming, less stressful and more effective. A proposed solution to this was the setting up of school consultation teams (see Figure 2.3).

These teams consisted of school representatives, normally the head or deputy and the SEN coordinator, representatives from the pupil support services attached to the school and other peripatetic personnel regularly involved in supporting the school. The latter group varied from school to school, including representatives from health (school nurse and speech therapist) and social services (Sure Start workers).

Problem solving within the school context

School consultation teams (SCTs) met twice a term in each school: at the first meeting to consider issues and to plan action, and at the second to review progress and refine action. Reports from these plan/action/review cycles were fed back to the ISS core group and provided the agenda for discussion at that group.

Evaluation data showed a very high level of satisfaction from the members of the SCT with strengths identified as:

- improved accessibility and contact with other professionals;
- improved clarity, focus and accountability in relation to children;
- opportunity for discussion/development of school policy;
- sharing of ideas/expertise;
- a forum for joint problem solving;
- widening perspectives/staff development;
- continuity when team membership changes;
- support/facilitation of inclusion projects.

The SCT resolved many of the difficulties of getting in touch with the support services, providing regular opportunities for contact with representatives from a range of relevant professional roles (see Figure 2.3). Much of the required communication could go on within the SCT meeting, but the meetings also enabled useful informal contact and easy opportunities for organizing joint case work. From the resulting multi-professional conversations a number of communication functions evolved that were not previously available.

One of these communication functions was the development of a commissioning process, whereby group members were able to decide between them who might be best able to support individual children of concern, thereby avoiding the parallel working that had occurred previously. The development of this commissioning function also had other unexpected communication functions. First, it allowed the SCTs to identify gaps in provision. Second, the group was alerted to the fact that, frequently, identified children were just representatives of a larger group who were emerging with similar, but not so severe, needs: the rest of the iceberg. This drew attention to the possibility of tailoring school/support services policies, in that particular school, to better meet the needs of this group, rather than creating an intervention for just the individual with the most obvious need.

These gaps, or needed developments, in provision could sometimes be dealt with by coordinated action by the SCT and sometimes were more appropriately referred to the core group for action at the level of the school partnership. As the records of the SCT meetings were considered at the core group meeting, issues and concerns were automatically taken forward.

Key functions of the integrated support service core group

The collating of evidence from the school consultation teams provided the core group with regular and comprehensive data about patterns of provision and school priorities, issues and concerns across the partnership.

Thus the core group had a clearing house function, receiving a continuous flow of information about the functioning of the support system on the ground, allowing core group members the opportunity to reflect on current practices and to be well informed in planning future action.

The ISS coordinator played a key role in the operation of this group, collating information from other forums to bring to the group, and taking forward proposed action. The coordinator was also influential in setting a problem solving and activist culture within the group so that there was a continual flow of projects being set up and evaluated to resolve issues raised by the school consultation teams. The core group prioritized actions in response to issues raised by a number of schools, but also supported individual school projects that were concerned with innovative inclusive practice.

Partnership-wide projects initiated by the core group included:

- addressing the concerns about improving communication with families through the development of the role of the home school community link worker;
- tackling the problem of the high number of children coming into school with language problems by collaborative school-based work with speech therapists;
- supporting newly qualified teachers with behaviour management strategies through partnership-wide staff development initiatives;
- resolving gaps in provision by sharing specialist resources across the partnership, for example additional behaviour support outreach and speech therapy;
- developing provision for managing crisis through the rapid response initiative – a multidisciplinary group that could be set up at a week's notice for managing complex cases (see Figure 2.3).

In addition, each school gave an example of an individual project to develop inclusive practice that had been supported to some degree by discussion in school consultation teams and the core group. Support included help in the formulation and/or the review of the project, and in some cases financial assistance from the core group. Head teachers stressed the value of support that could be quickly available to back initiatives to meet needs as they emerged.

Drawing on a full range of expert knowledge: linking multiprofessional networks

As the school consultation teams developed it became clear that some issues were difficult to resolve because of gaps in the areas of expertise held by the team. The two areas of particular concern related to child protection and mental health issues and it quickly became clear that representatives from these services would not be able to spare the time to be regular members of the SCTs. However, they could be represented in the core group and although the issues concerning mental health and social services were not completely resolved within the period of the evaluation, the involvement of the core group ensured that the issues were being dealt with at an appropriate strategic level and resulted in productive pilot work being put in place.

An example of such pilot work was the regular meetings between a member of social services and small groups of SEN coordinators. Each SEN coordinator would bring cases they were concerned about so that they were able to discuss levels of need and strategies for support and monitoring. As a result of this the SEN coordinators reported feeling much less stress about this area of their work and the social workers felt they were getting fewer and better referrals than before.

Changing the discourse: chasing resources to redeploying resources

There was nothing new in the practices that were developed in this partnership but there was a radical shift in how people working in the partnership felt about their work. Of the 40 people interviewed 39 described the working context provided by the school consultation teams as 'very good', and one person as 'good', in comparison to the entirely negative commentary of the previous study. Most significantly the discourse had shifted from the constant refrain of 'more resources' to a problem solving approach in the reconfiguration of the resourcing that was currently available. However, the EAZ status had brought a small purse with it. This paid for the 0.5 secondment for the core group coordinator and made a contribution to the employment of home school community link workers, providing a half share with each school. It also provided start-up funding for small projects in individual schools, supporting them in increasing their capacity to include vulnerable children.

Study 3: the rural context

Study 3 focused on a locality response to concerns similar to those identified in the baseline study (study 1). However, there were significant differences from the context reviewed in studies 1 and 2. First, the school partnership catchment area was a market town, providing a focus for a predominantly rural population that was above average in terms of socio-economic indicators. Levels of need were lower and there were substantially fewer resources compared to the school partnership in the urban studies. Second, it differed significantly from study 2 in being a grass-roots initiative starting with no additional initial funding or policy back-up. Third, again unlike study 2, it was a multiprofessional project from the beginning with significant participation from voluntary services, rather than being an interdisciplinary education project that invited in other agencies at a later stage in development (see Glenny 2000; Roaf 2002).

In the rural study there was a similar primary concern, as in the urban study, with getting together to share mutual concerns, but this time the solution was rather different. Instead of setting up a tight-knit core group, all those working with children and young people received an invitation to an open meeting entitled 'the Network'. The Network met twice a term for a one-hour meeting, and provided an open forum for informal discussion and the sharing of issues and concerns for interested field workers across agencies. Minutes were circulated to at least 60 people representing over 20 agency and community groups. The Network provided opportunities for discussion of key issues, for example sharing concerns about different professions' notions of confidentiality, and raising awareness of other agencies' roles, responsibilities and potential resources. The open and loose structure of the Network meetings allowed for fluidity in the membership and ensured all interested field workers in the area could attend.

Network discussions resulted in the identification of gaps in provision that were, in the first instance, responded to by individual agencies. An example of this was triggered by the identification of a small number of adolescents who were tying up education and social services resources. Discussion of this at the Network resulted in a local GP instigating a review of mental health services for young people in the area and the subsequent appointment of a clinical psychologist in his practice. This in turn offered parents more choice and released education and social services resources for work with other young people.

However, the size and loose organization of the Network meant that issues discussed were not always carried through into actions, particularly if action required interagency collaboration. Rather than losing the inclusiveness of the Network structure, the group proposed that a steering group should be set up to facilitate project development. Personnel for this group were drawn from interested members of the Network, ensuring representation from each of the key agencies and from partnership schools. With these two groups the Network had obtained a feedback loop of a different type from, but similar function to, the urban study (see Figure 2.4). And in the same way they used this structure to identify key issues that could be a focus of joint activity. Objectives identified at the time of the evaluation were:

- to focus on early intervention to raise achievement;
- to support good relationships between school and family life;
- to address the particular needs of a rural community distant from many city-based services;
- to seek solutions to gaps in provision identified through the Network and its members;
- to promote multiprofessional cooperation, training and information sharing.

To illustrate the nature of the operation of the Network across agency boundaries, a brief review of the Network response to the issue of early intervention follows.

Field workers interviewed illustrated how their given thresholds for involvement precluded being involved in early intervention. Shortage of resources in the services led to their work being largely crisis driven. Thus

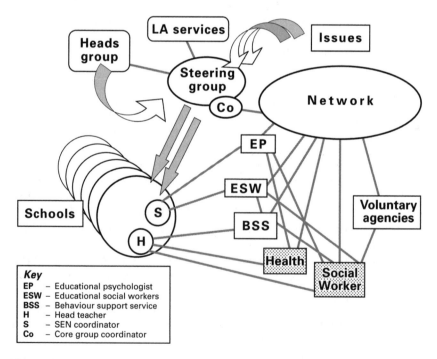

Figure 2.4 Communication systems: rural context, 'the Network'

while their personal view was that much of the work they did would have been more effective if they had intervened at an earlier stage, they were unable to justify intervention before critical indicators (for example, levels of absence from school) had been reached. Early intervention was also problematic from the point of view of gaining access to carry out sensitive work with young people and their families. Intervention from professionals in social work and education is often deemed to be threatening and therefore only justified in extremis. In the sessions observed, it was a key theme of the Network steering group to identify exactly what types of early intervention would be supportive and acceptable, and how these might be implemented. Issues discussed included:

- young people failing to attend therapy sessions because of transport difficulties;
- young people not having good access to information/support with health issues;
- difficulties in providing support for young people at transition/ stress points in their lives;
- difficulties in supporting young people and their families in the early stages of relationship breakdown (with school and/or family).

A range of solutions were suggested and a small grant from the Calouste Gulbenkian Foundation provided funds for project work prioritized by the Network. These were:

- funds to provide childcare and transport for parents having difficulties in taking their children to therapy sessions;
- support for the Bodyzone initiative, providing young people with regular access to health information and care on site at the secondary school (Harrison and Bullock 2005);
- the employment of a home school community link worker to work with vulnerable children/young people and their families.

Field workers subsequently interviewed described successful case examples of the use of all three initiatives. People who may not themselves have attended Network meetings, for example the head teachers interviewed, were able to identify significant benefits that had come from the Network and clearly saw its function as problem solving in orientation, resulting in a better use of existing special educational needs resources. Examples given of whole partnership projects included the effective training that resulted from a request from the heads' group to the steering group to improve the skills of learning support assistants (LSAs) in managing pupils with challenging behaviour; the development of a SEN coordinator forum; improved transition arrangements; the creation of a directory of resources for the area and the development of a resource centre for teachers and LSAs.

Overall there was clear evidence in the evaluation to show that the Network had generated multiprofessional solutions to problems that without the Network could have been seen as single agency quagmires.

In the following chapters we explore some of the implications of the findings of these case studies. Despite the rather different configurations to be found among the multiprofessional collaborations that were developing in the urban and rural contexts, there seemed to be some common underlying features. These are drawn out and discussed in Chapter 3.

3 Evolving a successful communication system

The key factor that we argue explains the success of the multiprofessional work in the urban and rural studies outlined in Chapter 2 is the nature of the communication system in which individual case work was embedded. In this chapter we explore the characteristics of these two, differently configured, communication systems, compare the findings of the studies reported in Chapter 2 with other research exploring multiprofessional partnerships, and draw out common principles that seem to underpin effective communication systems.

In each study, the first step to improve multiprofessional collaboration was to build a reflective capacity into the existing organizational structures. In the urban study this was through the *core group*, a representative sample of local practitioners, and in the rural study through the *Network*, an open meeting for any local practitioner who wished to attend. In each case, these groups provided a viewing platform to make visible the complex interactions that made up the work in a given patch.

With this reflective capacity, the practitioners and managers in each local area had quality information about the dynamics of their particular patch. This provided them with the feedback to improve the performance of their joint activity by both refining their communication systems and developing their practice. The urban and rural studies provide examples of both. Thus field workers within the organization are in a position to identify strengths and to ensure they are acknowledged and enhanced. Similarly, they can explore and prioritize improvement in areas of weakness/dysfunction in the system and develop strategies to improve them.

Vickers ([1965] 1995), writing in the 1960s on his experience of working across civil service departments, describes the development of similar types of communication networks, which he refers to as *appreciative systems*. He used the word *appreciative* to draw attention to the importance of reading the detail of what was happening in a given organization and through so doing, drawing on and responding to the contributions and experiences of the organization's members. He points out that groups of people working together inevitably create a system of relationships that both supports and constrains them. He saw these systems as self-organizing: the system 'if left alone ... will regulate itself' (p. 43). He observed that this 'self-organization' creates a context that effectively controls the people working within the organization, especially if they do not themselves understand the dynamics that are being created around them. This explains the findings in the baseline study where respondents felt themselves to be enmeshed in a system that 'wasn't working'.

This raises questions about who or what 'the system' is and how it can self-organize. The individuals who feel enmeshed in the system are the elements that enmesh, so how do they contribute to the creation of a context that they then experience as so constraining? The systems of relationships that develop between groups of people in complex organizations, seem to get laid down according to a rule of finding the shortest route. As at Sussex University campus, where no paths were designed until the campus had been used for a while so that the laying of paths could follow the journeys people were typically taking, the system of relationships is built by the accretions of the historical use of the system. For example, in the baseline study, school staff had little time to spend on chasing support, and therefore services which were difficult to access were bypassed and other solutions to the problems were found. Thus schools were frequently referring children on the basis of availability of services, rather than on the basis of the best fit to need. Such behaviour became an irritant, resulting in resistance on the part of services to whom referral was being made. In order to protect themselves from inappropriate referrals, services tightened their entry criteria thereby reducing the flow of communication and the access to resources.

At certain points in the development of the system national solutions further sculpt the territory, for example the setting up of 'statementing' procedures, the costs and problems of which have already been discussed in Chapter 2. In order to be fair and allocate resources to the most needy, systems were set up which consumed a large part of the resource. This resulted in distortions to the support system, with large parts of the system organizing around a paperchase to obtain the visible resource, while at the same time substantially reducing the amount of resource available. The result of this was a system that was always orientated towards pulling in something from the outside rather than reflecting upon the best use of what was readily available. Indeed, much of what was readily available was being used to pull in resources from the outside.

Thus the actions of uncoordinated individuals and small groups interacting with national policies set up channels that direct the flow of subsequent action. As these patterns emerge they create expectations in the minds of other members of the organization, who also start to behave in the same way, and the channels deepen. As the channels deepen it becomes increasingly difficult to take alternative routes. Past behaviour comes to control and limit future behaviour.

An important difference between the laying out of paths at Sussex University and the system of relationships that emerges in loose-knit multiprofessional organizations, is in the stability of the organizations. At Sussex University the buildings remain constant over time, and when changes occur they are visible and can be planned for. In the case of multiprofessional communication systems, there is rarely a map of the formal routes, and certainly not of the many informal routes. Essentially the system is invisible, and only becomes visible, and then only in part, when it is felt not to be working. Further, it is much more volatile than a campus route map: new people, new services and new national priorities are continually causing changes to the systems of relationships. If these are not being continuously monitored and adaptations made, then the multiprofessional project is flying blind, as could be seen in the baseline study in Chapter 2, while in the urban and rural studies the multi-professional work was embedded in an *appreciative system*.

What are the conditions necessary to setting up an appreciative system?

Shared purposes

Vickers identified that agreeing and maintaining project purpose was a major problem when working across different departments. Individual department outcomes were frequently formed in isolation despite the fact that the implications of their actions could cut across policy in departments with related concerns. Further that the interactions of policy initiatives were so unpredictable that, even if joint policy were developed, the effects could only really be measured when they were worked through in practice.

Thus, Vickers argued, in order to maintain purpose the system required a self-steering mechanism that would record vital indicators and continually make small adjustments to policies to maintain the right course. In the case of multiprofessional services for children, the right course is itself contested, and different services make different decisions about appropriate working practices and resource allocation. Thus, agreeing the right course, or project purpose, would seem to be an essential prerequisite to effective joint action.

However, Huxham and Vangen (2005) counsel against getting too bogged down in the details of agreement of joint purpose. In their extensive review of partnerships in a range of organizational contexts, they found that successful partnerships were most likely to develop from relatively small collaborations around issues of mutual interest that then grew as the organizations began to trust each other. They found that heavily managed collaborations, where a lot of time was spent on the 'rules of engagement', often resulted in what they describe as *collaborative inertia*. That is, the costs of collaboration, for example the time spent in meetings and on retraining programmes, outweighed the value of any visible outcomes for the participants. Indeed, Huxham and Vangen argue that collaborative working is always expensive in resources and what they call *collaborative advantage* is only really achieved when the collaboration is absolutely necessary.

So how can shared purpose be achieved without enduring collaborative inertia? One feature of both the urban and the rural study was the maintenance of a clear focus to the projects. This could be interpreted as, 'How can services in this geographical area, be supported in providing the best possible educational opportunities for their most vulnerable and disaffected members?' However, as Huxham and Vangen had found in their review, these projects had not included any time spent on developing a common mission statement, but rather had begun their collaborative relationship by trying to resolve a present and practical problem. In the urban study this had been concerned with improving access to support services, and in the rural study it had been a discussion of the barriers to communication presented by different notions of confidentiality.

Thus, shared purpose had been negotiated over time as a result of working together successfully. Working together successfully had been achieved through collaboration on small resolvable pieces of work of direct concern to everybody involved. Collaborative advantage had been achieved because all participants could see the relevance of their joint working, and their joint actions had resulted in visible improvements in the short term. So shared purpose seems to be a function of shared activity, rather than a prerequisite to it. The galvanizing feature, then, seems to be shared activity – but shared activity is itself a function of the opportunity for joint working, so what facilitates joint working?

Opportunities for joint working

One feature of the evaluation studies that both writers have been involved in over the last ten years (Glenny 2000, 2001, 2005a, 2007a, b; Roof 2002) is the large number of examples of good quality work with children and families coming out of informal collaborations between field workers on the ground. The nature of these relationships will be more fully examined in Chapter 4. However, the relationships happened because of the proximity of the field workers: they were regularly involved with the same children and families, on the same 'patch'. Similarly the multiprofessional communication systems that were examined in the urban and rural studies were based in particular and bounded geographical areas. In both of these cases the patch consisted of a secondary school and feeder primaries.

This raises the question of how a 'patch' can be created. Is there an optimum size to achieve a sense of place and a feeling of belonging that disappears if the local area becomes too large? At the same time, is there a minimum size, perhaps limited by levels of resources? Does the services notion of 'patch' relate to some sense of community membership in the minds of the children, young people and their families who are being served?

In a follow-up study to those described in the previous chapter (Glenny 2005a), comparing the services for children and their families in six localities, there were examples of areas of different sizes and areas of different type, for example parts of cities and large rural areas focused on county towns. Two of the six localities were the urban and rural studies considered in Chapter 2, but now three years older as working systems. The local authority in which all six localities were placed had a history of supporting schools in working in partnerships and this had been important in defining the patches that emerged in the studies reported in Chapter 2. Of the six localities, there were four for which the data suggested field workers were content with their patch and two that seemed to be experiencing problems that related to the geography of the locality.

Of the contented localities, size varied from one locality in a high need area, comprising part of a secondary catchment area that supported two primary schools and a children's centre, to a county town and surrounding villages, with two large secondary schools and feeder primaries, and two children's centres. Of those experiencing difficulties, one was a collection of high need areas where services had not historically been congruent, and one was the urban study reviewed in Chapter 2, based on two geographically coherent estates but which had now been expanded to include neighbouring areas of high need. The neighbouring areas were not in themselves coherent localities and the newly formed locality cut across community boundaries. In both cases it was perceived to be difficult to make decisions at core group meetings because they were missing key personnel or alternatively covering issues that were not sufficiently relevant to group members. Thus in both localities the costs of collaboration seemed to be often outweighing the benefits, so that the group was experiencing what Huxham and Vangen have called *collaborative inertia*. In the urban study, this was in strict contrast to the very positive experiences of meetings reported in the original study three years earlier. From this evidence, we make the tentative assumption that the geographical features of the 'patch' are significant in determining the functionality of the communication system that serves it.

Minding the system

Thus the successful localities, although differently configured, had some underlying similarities. They had an appreciative system which seemed to be serving a common purpose. The practitioners in schools and children's services had opportunities to discuss and communicate about their activities, and this was made possible because of a shared geographical location or patch. However, all of these common aspects required maintenance, and in each of the successful areas in the six localities study, the systems were being carefully 'minded', that is, an individual or small group was clearly assigned to ensuring the maintenance of the fragile and complex network of relationships that makes up an appreciative system.

The issue of maintenance is also a clear feature of other studies of partnership working. Huxham and Vangen (2005: 80) report on the results of collaborative partnerships between a whole range of organizations and conclude:

> The nurturing process must be continuous and permanent ... what we mean by nurturing is a continual focus on actively managing the collaboration ... implied in this is an expectation that a collaboration is unlikely to be self sustaining so there is a requirement for constant attention to keep it from spiraling into decline ...

In the baseline study, no one was attending to the system, it had been left in Vickers' words to 'self-organize'. In the urban and rural studies and in the successful areas in the six localities study, the 'minder' role was clearly evident, and distinctive in being rather unlike typical notions of leadership and coordination. For this reason the term 'system minder' was coined, to aid in the analysis of the specific skills involved.

What kind of role did the system minder play?

An analysis of the tasks carried out by the system minder in the urban and rural studies demonstrated the following key roles:

- guarding project purpose;
- 'norm holding';
- receiving issues and concerns;
- monitoring task completion;
- orchestrating relationships and overseeing communication across the related communication structures in a given locality.

Guarding project purpose

One important feature of the system minder observed in all the successful localities was to hold the ring in relation to the history of the development of the appreciative system. With regular changes in membership the *system minder* acts to focus the collective memory of the group, so that the discussion of issues can move forward and norms that evolve through the developing experience of the group, can be maintained: '... because of the dynamics of intention among these individuals, a system emerges ... they may not remember why or how the organization first occurred or why the given organizational structure is chosen over other possible forms' (Marion 1999: 29).

The holding of the collective memory avoids the feeling of 'groundhog day' that is characteristic of many loose-knit organizational structures, where ways of working are endlessly re-discussed as group membership changes. At the same time, it was not the role of the minder to have the vision or take a lead in developing the direction of the group. The minder was there to ensure that the group was helped towards a developing consensus, and that this was faithfully represented and maintained. For this reason the role could be problematic for people who had been in traditional leadership roles. People who had been used to exercising what Handy (1990) refers to as 'positional power' tended to short-cut the process of gaining consensus in order to move things on in their own preferred direction. At the same time they also tended to be more conscious of the hierarchical structures in which they found themselves so that their attention was drawn to mediating the external drivers at the expense of the voice of the group they were representing. Both of these behaviours distracted them from representing the group and distorted the channels of communication.

The really effective 'system minders' had what Handy refers to as 'relational' power, they had the respect of their colleagues usually built up through local knowledge and joint working on the ground over a period of time. They held tenaciously to the role of facilitating and representing the group, thereby supporting the group in defining its identity and pursuing its core goals. They held a neutral stance so that their own perspectives were not privileged by their position. They functioned to support the group to reflect upon their purposes, processes and practices and to continually make small adjustments, to evolve towards a best fit between available resources and local needs.

Norm holding

If holding the ring was one aspect of maintaining project purpose, then an equally important one was a continuous monitoring of the playing out of roles and responsibilities within the group. There were many examples, in the successful localities, of small interventions and adjustments made by the system minder that prevented the 'spiralling into decline' that Huxham and Vangen (2005) describe. For example, an educational social worker (ESW) was expressing frustration about the amount of her time that was being spent in school consultation team meetings, when she felt she needed more time for her case work. The system minder was able to get a review of her work and reduce the number of school consultation teams she attended. At the same time the system minder was able to tell the ESW about feedback received from other group members about how much they had valued her contribution, because of her experience and her knowledge of families in the locality. Having her concerns responded to and understanding that there was a value for other people in her attendance at the meeting, the ESW continued to attend regularly and without further complaint. This kind of intervention seems trivial but attendance at the school consultation teams is essential to their survival. If particular field workers fail to attend, the value of the meeting is diminished for everybody and other field workers begin to question why they are making the time.

Similarly, head teachers would describe how they had thought about cancelling school consultation team meetings because of other pressures but had not done so because they knew the system minder would be asking them about how the meeting had gone. Cancelling the meeting would have serious consequences because of the difficulty of getting another date that everybody could make. In both cases the system minder had supported colleagues in 'norm holding', that is, gently ensuring that the necessary behaviours had been maintained, for the ongoing health of an *appreciative system*.

Discussing the role of the school consultation team with colleagues in other authorities, we had been surprised to find that they had tried school consultation teams and they hadn't worked. The reasons for not working were all issues raised in the localities we observed, but had been left untreated because there was no one minding the system. In contrast, the school consultation teams which were part of the urban study were still very highly rated after five years of operation because the 'norm holding' had resulted in viable and productive meetings.

Receiving issues and concerns

Another feature of the system minder was their availability for informal dialogue about issues of concern. The system minder's role was not to resolve the issues, but rather to ensure the issues got a hearing. In some cases the system minder would be able to link the person with the issue, to work that was already going on in the locality that they were just unaware of. In other cases they would add the issue to the relevant agenda, for example in the urban study to the core group or the school consultation team, and in the rural study to the Network meeting or the working group.

A crucial aspect of this role was that everybody within the system felt it was worth sharing issues with the system minder, because if the issues were not shared and dealt with they could become a focus for problems later. For example, a school representative explained to the system minder that there was no point in bringing social care issues to the school consultation team meeting, even though they were her greatest current concern, because there were no social workers at the meeting. However, by not bringing these issues to the meeting, an issue for the appreciative system was not being aired and therefore could not be worked upon. By encouraging the airing of seemingly irresolvable issues, the group can start to find solutions. Further, the more apparently irresolvable the issues, the more crucial it is for them to be explored as they are likely to be causing the most problems to the most people and hence these are often referred to as *wicked issues* (Hodgkin and Newell 1996: 32).

Interestingly, in the data from the baseline study, these were precisely the issues to which solutions were not being sought: they were seen as 'the way things are' or that 'have to be lived with'. Often this was associated with the idea that it was another agency's domain and therefore not territory that could be trod. Goldratt (1990), as a consultant working with businesses to optimize their organizations, has referred to these issues as the *constraints* in the system. Goldratt's *theory of constraints* rests on his findings that the most problematic constraint seriously depletes the resources of the whole organization and needs to be resolved, and when it is resolved, attention can be given to the next most problematic constraint and so on. The theory of constraints includes a set of tools to identify the most constraining of these *wicked issues* in order to focus available energy on resolving them.

The application of the *theory of constraints* is a challenge in a multiprofessional context, and emphasizes the need to bring wicked issues to the surface in order to resolve them. Thus, again, the system minder role becomes key in engendering trust, taking a neutral, non-judgemental position and being available to all the participants within the system in order for the free flow of information to occur.

Monitoring task completion

In principle, monitoring task completion involved ensuring the various groups that made up the system, completed the tasks they set themselves. In reality the 'system minder' spent a lot of time on chasing up, servicing meetings, freeing up communication links and ensuring the business of the group was taking place efficiently. In particular, keeping costly multiprofessional meetings to a minimum by ensuring the work commissioned by the meeting had progressed by the next meeting. This included ensuring meetings were chaired successfully. Through an effective chair, issues raised in meetings were brought to some kind of stage in the resolution process, or working parties were set up, so that the work required to resolve them could be taken forward by the next meeting.

Orchestrating relationships and overseeing communication across the related communication structures in a given locality

Finally, the system minder at the centre of the communication system had a good view of how effectively it was functioning, providing information to the relevant groups as to what could be done to optimize its functioning and ensure that meeting time was kept to a minimum. The system minder was also in a good position to provide information to support the process of auditing resources and evaluating service provision. For example, in one local area the system minder had facilitated the setting up of a forum for children and young people drawing on the school councils in the area. In another, the system minder had linked to regular parents forum meetings at the local children's centre to provide feedback on aspects of service provision. In each case the feedback was used to inform discussion in the multi-professional forum and, in effect, extended the communication system to include the perspectives of service users.

Managing complexity

What is interesting about the urban and rural studies is that they have been generated by local action, as indeed had the examples of multiprofessional projects discussed by Roaf (2002). On first analysis this seemed to be incidental: local people had developed these ideas but the principles that underpinned these projects could be described, and therefore it should be possible to recreate them elsewhere. However, findings from the study of six localities (Glenny 2005a) suggest that this may not be so easy to achieve. The localities were successful almost in direct proportion to the extent that they were locally initiated. The one that was the least successful was the only one that was initiated from the centre.

At the same time, as was discussed in Chapter 1, despite endless policy objectives, multiprofessional working in general seems to be very difficult to organize. Why might it be the case that local organization can be effective but is difficult to replicate on a bigger scale? A possible answer is that complex organizational structures are not amenable to traditional top-down management approaches. Rihani (2005) uses an analogy to suggest why. A senior manager in the health service had suggested to Rihani that leading the health service was like being the captain of an ocean liner, a steer to the left and the ship and all its members went to the left. Rihani questioned this analogy and suggested that in fact leading the health service was more akin to being the lead fish in a shoal. In a shoal, a large group immediately behind you would follow you, particularly those with a high investment in being seen to tuck in, but much of the following shoal could shear off and follow their own purposes.

In our studies, individual interview data with field workers provided examples of shearing off from the main shoal for a variety of different reasons. A number of respondents talked about operating 'below the radar', particularly in contexts where restructuring was taking place. They were seen by their managers as being 'resistant to change', but saw themselves as protecting local relationships and projects that had taken time to establish and were in danger of being washed away by the restructuring process. This kind of alternative perspective emerges because it is impossible for senior managers, operating a top-down model, to get the view of the system necessary to see what is happening on the ground. At the same time even if they did take the time necessary to have a different vantage point, the complexity of what they saw, would be difficult for them to parse. The non-linear nature of the relationships within the system means that when changes are made, the results are not predictable. For each intended aim there are a number of unintended consequences, and these consequences are likely to undermine the morale of those people who are required to implement the changes. So how can these complex organizations be managed more effectively?

Drawing from complexity theory

Non-linear situations exist when a given cause may lead to more than one outcome, and if the process were repeated the results could be, and often are, different. These non-linear relationships are typical of complex systems and a body of work is developing to analyse the dynamics of these systems when they occur as either natural or social phenomena. This body of work is loosely organized under the headings of complexity theory or the complexity sciences and derives from chaos theory. Rihani and Geyer (2001) discuss the emergence of the 'non-linear paradigm' drawing on contributions from its formulation in mathematics, biology and meteorology (discussed, for example, by Lewin 1993, and Buchanan 2002) as well as more recent application in the social sciences (for example, Stacey 2001). The classic example of this kind of system was originally described by meteorologists attempting to explain the unpredictability of weather systems and has come to be known as the 'butterfly effect': a butterfly flaps its wings over the Amazon rain forest causing turbulence which, amplified by particular atmospheric conditions, sets in motion events that lead to a storm over Chicago. The following day the same butterfly, behaving in the same way, has no effect on the weather system.

The butterfly effect is not just an analogy but a mathematical possibility, reflecting the dynamics of the weather system and the key features of a complex system. A complex system is made up of lots of small units of interaction. These units of interaction both provide a context for the interactions of others and are themselves influenced by the context in which they occur. Complexity theorists argue that these relationships can co-exist in a number of different states of which the main themes are *order*, *chaos* and *self-organized complexity*. To explain these differences Kauffman (1995a: 20) gives the example of water in a bath. With tap and plug closed, the water is in a state of order. With the tap running, the water is chaotic, but with the tap running at a steady speed and the plug removed, the water quickly patterns itself into what is known as a stable vortex, an example of self-organization. Holland (1998: 7) takes the water metaphor further to explore the transitory role of individual interactions in the continuation of these self-organizing patterns:

mechanisms themselves modify the pattern of interactions, through adaptation to each other ... emergence usually involves patterns of interaction that persist despite a continual turn over in the constituents of the patterns ... A simple example is the standing wave in front of a rock in a white-water river. The water molecules making up the wave change instant by instant, but the wave persists as long as the rock is there and the water flows ...

Returning to our butterfly, the interactions between its movement and the context within which it is moving can cause *amplification* of its movement, be *neutral* in relation to its movement or *attenuate* its movement, in each case causing it to affect the context in which it finds itself to a greater or lesser degree. Similarly, people in relationships influence the outcomes of the actions of those around them. The same thing said by a high-status person and a low-status person may be heard very differently. Joint action can have very different outcomes according to the trust between the different people involved. Status and trust are just two possible variables that can cause significant amplification and attenuation of the messages being communicated between members of a system.

Systems may also be shaped by features of the landscape in which the patterns of individual interaction are taking place. In Kauffman's example of the bath water, gravity was operating on the interacting water molecules to draw them down the plug hole, and in so doing was operating as an *attractor* in the system, strongly influencing the particular configurations the water molecules would make. Similarly, as discussed earlier in this chapter, statementing procedures were acting as an attractor in the system, drawing in a lot of individual effort as a perceived solution to achieving resources, causing the system to configure itself in particular ways that were ultimately counter-productive.

Kauffman (1993) modelled the actions of these complex systems by running computer simulations of multiple entities interacting, with their interactions governed by simple rule systems. He found that over time the patterns of interactions evolved with an overall effect of optimizing the whole system to provide a better fit with a particular environment. Such evolving systems, within the framework of complexity theory, are known as *complex adaptive systems*. They have this adaptive property because of what is known as the *emergent* features of the system. That is, in particular contexts, the interactions throw up new *emergent* features which survive if they help the overall system to configure itself more effectively in relation to a given environment. At the same time other emergent properties will be lost because they give no global advantage.

Kauffman's examples were very simple simulations but the principle has since been frequently observed in complex systems: 'In both biology and technology, adaptation can be seen as an attempt to optimize systems riddled with conflicting constraints' (1995b: 119). By adaptation, Kauffman means, the gradual evolution of complex structures as they are subjected to small changes to provide a best fit for their environment. He gives the example of the development of the bicycle, beginning with a range of what now seem eccentric configurations, in an attempt to resolve the conflicting constraints of comfort and speed. Bicycle design eventually settled down into two or three similar types of design, each version a best fit for particular purposes, a hegemony only disrupted when a new material becomes available, with new characteristics of, for example, strength or weight, offering possibilities not so far considered. 'Conflicting constraints' are an inevitable feature of complex organizations, and, as such, solutions fluctuate in order to better meet one constraint and then the other, until an optimum solution is achieved. Such evolution can not occur by implementing sudden structural change, to meet a grand plan, disrupting the relationships and processes negotiated together over time. The solutions to complexity can only be met by gradual incremental change, building on the structures and relationships that are already in place.

This notion of adaptation is being increasingly discussed as having application to human organizations (for example, Stacey 2001). However, the application to human organizations is difficult to follow through because human organizations are rarely left alone to evolve in particular environments as in the biological examples, or to meet relatively clear-cut purposes as in the technological examples. In human organizations the interactive elements are themselves making conscious choices and these choices are more or less relevant depending on the relative power that they hold. However, despite these differences there do seem to be similarities between Vickers' account of an appreciative system, the findings of the evolving structures in the urban and rural case studies, and the idea of *complex adaptive systems*.

Further, the key ideas that shape *complex adaptive systems* – the importance of attending to the dynamics created by the multiple interactions in the system; identifying *attractors* that may be very influential in configuring or distorting the system; the notions of *amplification* and *attenuation* of communication; and the concept of *emergence* – all seem to be useful tools for exploring multiprofessional communication systems. Complexity theory provides a framework for analysing complex dynamic systems that have non-linear relationships between inputs and outputs and the power relations that operate within those systems. The lessons from a complexity analysis are that:

- it is not possible to predict the outcomes of actions in complex contexts; thus
- decision making can only be successful if it is continually attentive to sensitive feedback systems; and
- if the changes are small so that their impact, and in particular unintended consequences, can be monitored.

Because the multiprofessional groups in the urban and rural case studies were not centrally directed, their only options were to work more effectively with what they had, and in order to do this they needed to audit their current functioning. Following on from this audit they made small incremental changes to the system as they had the energy to do so. Thus precisely because of the constraints they were working within, they stumbled across a complex adaptive system.

Size does matter

The size of the locality to be served by such a system has also come up as an issue in our earlier discussion of successful systems. Marion (1999: 95), in a discussion of the relationship between the size and complexity of organizations, concludes: 'If the system is particularly complex, the constraints may defy any solution, and the system must reduce its complexity before it can expect to achieve fitness.'

Stacey (2001: 177) draws on Kauffman's simulation studies to shed light on why this might be:

> Kauffman's simulations show ... when the number of connections between agents is small, the dynamics take the form of stability, that is highly repetitive patterns of behaviour. This happens because small numbers of connections mean the constraints agents impose on each other are few. When the number of connections is very high, the dynamics are highly unstable because the conflicting constraints agents impose on each other are numerous, but at a critical number of connections, neither too few nor too many, the dynamics at 'the edge of chaos' arises, which is neither stable enough to obstruct the potential for change nor so unstable as to destroy pattern ...

So Stacey finds not just an explanation for critical size in complex organizations but also an implication that size is linked to the potential for creative meaning making. He goes on to present Kauffman's argument that optimum size is often naturally achieved by large organizations breaking down into what he calls 'patches': '... Patching reduces the number of connections across the whole system and so tends to stabilize it enough to avoid the destructiveness of highly unstable dynamics ... Patches are not organized but spontaneously emerge ...' (Stacey 2001: 177).

Kauffman's (2005a) findings that these patches spontaneously emerge, again draws attention to the importance of carefully auditing what is currently happening to ensure the developing policy builds on what has already fruitfully evolved.

Power relations

A complexity analysis thus provides a possible account of why over-assertion of top-down management structures are unlikely to facilitate multiprofessional working. A multiprofessional context is inevitably complex. As a complex set of relationships it will self-organize into a system of communication and practice that will provide the context for the work of all its members. This system can be visible or invisible to its members. If it is invisible then its members will experience its constraining aspects without being able to take any kind of control. If it can be made visible, it can effectively become an 'appreciative system', and then its members are able to harness the information it holds and evolve its structure and functioning to better achieve their aims. Crucially, the development of these strategies takes place from the perspective of members of the whole organization reflecting on their joint activities, not from the point of view of one part of the organization, for example a senior managers' group or an individual service, deciding for change. Thus everybody has access to the reasons for change and the rationale for a particular approach to that change.

Further, these appreciative systems seem to have size limitations, and thus in a given local authority there may need to be a number of appreciative systems focusing on services to children, young people and their families. Kauffman's (1995a) simulations lead him to propose that the size of these systems is critically determined by the number and nature of the interactions that take place within the system. The evidence from our studies suggests a similar optimum geographical area, depending on notions of community and numbers and levels of interactions.

The examples from the successful locality studies suggest that networked communication can provide an appreciative system and this can be locally monitored by a system minder. Further, that these 'appreciative' communication systems can build on each other: the school consultation team feeding into the locality core group or network, which then feeds into the area groups that inform local authority strategy. Thus it follows that good decision making in a local authority, will be informed by the feedback generated by these collections of appreciative systems. Indeed, decision making at local authority level needs to look after the needs of these 'appreciative systems' and will depend on the knowledge they provide.

The findings we have described using a complexity analysis have similar implications to those that come from what is known in the organizational literature as 'structural contingency theory'. This theory identifies that the efficiency of an organization is dependent on the relationship between the form of the organization and the environment in which it finds itself:

> An organization can be integrated either by plan (rules, goals, standardized procedures, or outputs) or by feedback (communication, continual adaptation, or updating). If environmental demands are relatively stable, if outcomes can be predicted, then co-ordination or plan will suffice ... highly differentiated organizations in volatile environments, by contrast, must be co-ordinated by feedback.
>
> (Marion 1999: 85)

Clearly, loose-knit multiprofessional systems come into the latter category.

In the next chapter, we consider research on the role of the home school community link worker. The link workers provide an example of a role that has emerged from local concerns about gaps in provision. The evaluation draws attention to the importance of the quality of relationships in the successful functioning of the support services. Through the presentation of data from the evaluation, parents and carers provide a commentary on their experience of the support system as a whole – and indeed how, in Sen's (1999) phrase, 'the direction of public policy can be influenced by the effective use of participatory capabilities by the public' (p. 18).

4 Customizing provision to meet local needs

The 'appreciative systems' described in the last chapter provide an appropriate environment in which to review how field workers in a locality are being deployed, and to reconfigure the work of those field workers to better meet the identified needs of the children and families that are being served. Examples of such reconfiguration and changing practice can be seen in the case studies discussed in Chapter 2. For example, the adoption of school consultation team meetings and informal social work support in the urban study and the development of mental and general health provision in the rural study. At the same time, gaps in provision were identified that could not easily be met by current field workers working differently. More seriously, the gaps in provision were only being identified by service providers; the voice of the user is not represented in the decision making processes discussed so far. This chapter looks at a particular example of an emerging role designed to fill these gaps in provision and looks in detail at user perspectives on this new role. In so doing we hope to shed some light on how services can customize their provision to better support children, young people and their families in a particular locality, and to examine how user perspectives can be made integral to these decision making processes.

The gaps in provision most frequently identified were in relation to the need for earlier intervention. Field workers interviewed (Glenny 2000, 2001), described how they were precluded from working with children at a point where needs were clearly evident, by the thresholds that triggered their involvement. Thus, while their personal view was that much of the work they did would have been more effective if they had intervened at an earlier stage, they were unable to justify intervention before critical indicators (for example levels of absence from school) had been reached. Because of the statutory responsibilities that came with their involvement, their services were also frequently viewed with alarm by children and families who experienced the contact as stigmatizing, thereby reducing the likelihood of a successful relationship being established. At the same time, as we have discussed in Chapter 2, schools were very much concerned about the children they were identifying as in need of more support than they felt able to offer, whom they were trying to manage for considerable periods of time, before further support could be triggered.

This focus on early intervention generated significant discussion in all the multiprofessional forums studied. Typical concerns included:

- the need for improvements in communication between home and school;
- the loss of service provision because young people were failing to attend therapy sessions;
- the difficulties in providing support for young people at stress points in their lives, for example at transitions;
- the lack of resources for supporting young people and their families in the early stages of relationship breakdown (with school and/or family);
- the need for more support for parents who for a range of reasons were struggling to meet the demands of parenting.

In both the urban and the rural study, discussion around meeting these needs led to the emergence of a new type of support, that of the home school community link worker (also referred to from here on as the link worker). In the urban study, this role was partly financed by schools, supported by funding from the local education action zone (EAZ). In the rural study, the network steering group successfully achieved independent funding for the setting up of the role. In both projects the role was perceived by service providers to be a very effective addition to the system of support for children and families (Glenny 2000; Roaf 2002) and influenced the development of similar provision in other parts of the local authority.

The link workers, differently configured to support two rather different populations, had emerged as an important role in both localities. The significance of the role seemed to be in the capacity of the workers to bridge the gap that had developed between the reach of the universal services and the support provided by specialist services. With the coming of the Children's Fund in 2003 (a source of new money specifically targeting early intervention) a number of localities bid for Children's Fund money to set up similar provision in their areas. The local Children's Fund was keen to support such bids as national experience (Webb and Vulliamy 2004) had also shown the value of the link worker role. The subsequent evaluation (Glenny 2007a) will be discussed here to explore why the role was seen to be so valuable.

The evaluation began in September 2004, and was completed in

March 2007. There were ten link workers employed in six pilot areas and each worker was interviewed two or three times over the period of the study. Thirty case studies were drawn from this interview process. For each case study, evidence was sought from other people working with the families, and where possible, from the parents and children who were receiving the service. Twenty parent interviews were conducted (5 face-to-face and 15 by phone) and short questionnaire feedback was achieved from a further ten parents. General data on the effectiveness of the service were drawn from interviews with co-workers, observation of steering group meetings and training sessions.

The role of the home school community link worker

The workers in the Children's Fund project were not just involved with linking the school and the home but also had a wider community role, including providing support after school and during school holiday periods. For this reason they were entitled home school community link workers. The work with families invariably began with the development of a relationship and the building of trust. This seemed to be the defining feature of the way in which the link workers supported families and they were prepared to spend time on this process. It was a very noticeable feature of the case studies that families that had seemed difficult to engage in year one, made heavy demands on the workers in year two but required much less support in year three as they were able to link independently into other resources, and in particular, children's centres (see Table 4.1 for case study data).

While there were some differences in approach, all the link workers sought to normalize their work with families as much as possible, helping parents and children to 'move on' through practical help in sorting problems and linking into other specialist and community resources. As one link worker expressed it:

> ... we can be helping with things that are quite minor, but in so doing, linking people back into the community, helping parents to join in with their children, not being stigmatized around working with people who need help – you can shoot yourself in the foot if you are seen as a problem person ...

This low-key approach was also evident in parents' view of the role. Two parents expressed the following views: '... it was like having my mother to talk to ...'; and '... she is like a big sister ... or perhaps a nice auntie ...'.

The elements of the role itemized below are drawn from the 30 case studies and are classified under the headings of the *Every Child Matters* five outcomes for children. All the case studies demonstrated more than one 'intervention'. Indeed, typically there was a range of types of support offered, and over the period of the relationship with the family, these were modified to best meet the family's changing needs.

Being healthy: physical and mental

- individual support for children, e.g. regarding parental illness/ addiction;
- signposting and supporting links to other resources, e.g. young carers and mental health groups;
- supporting parents with parenting issues;
- supporting the siblings of children who have high-level needs (involved with other services);
- working with the family to problem solve in order to build independence;
- helping parents and children through family crisis, e.g. illness/ marriage breakdown/bereavement;
- supporting parents in building confidence to attend support groups.

Staying safe: protection from harm and neglect

- working alongside social work/behaviour support workers/mental health workers to provide continuity/ongoing support;
- supporting families while they were experiencing statutory interventions, e.g. exclusion/child protection/court procedures;
- supporting attendance at appointments, e.g. mental health clinics/speech therapy;
- alerting the support networks to gain support to meet identified needs;
- acting as an early warning system to alert other services to child protection issues.

Enjoying and achieving: education, training and recreation

- building relationships with school – parents being 'heard' and having more 'say' in decision making and as a result engaging more fully in their children's education;
- helping schools to fully appreciate the issues for children and

families, so that they can provide appropriate opportunities for children;

- group work for parents on supporting their children's education;
- running primary secondary transition groups for vulnerable children;
- taking children/parents out because they need a break;
- running customized 'fun days' in the vacation for groups of children;
- linking to local community resources for young people, e.g. sports training;
- achieving charity funding to support children *in extremis*, e.g. adventure holidays/music lessons.

Making a positive contribution

- individual counselling to build self-esteem/empowerment;
- group work with children to develop relationship skills and to develop the capacity to support each other.

Economic well-being

- helping through family crisis, e.g. marriage breakdown/debt/ poor housing;
- linking parents to other resources, e.g. debt counselling/housing department/charity funding;
- supporting parents in achieving their rights, e.g., through helping with the completion of complex procedures such as disability living allowance applications;
- building parents' confidence to enable them to take up opportunities for training, life skills and/or work;
- signposting parents to training and work opportunities.

Link workers supported different numbers of schools (ranging from one to eight) and were employed for different amounts of time with contracts sometimes restricted to term time and sometimes extending over holiday periods. Workload also built up as the role became established, and this resulted in changing priorities. In particular there was a shift from working with children to working with parents as the case load of family work increased. After a year in the role, one full-time link worker, working with two primary and one secondary school in a high-need area, was supporting between 40 and 50 children, with a 50 per cent turnover over the course of the year, and 35–40 parents. Of the children, 40 per cent were girls and 60 per cent were boys; 30 per cent were from the secondary and

70 per cent from the primary schools. The figures include individual and group work with both children and parents.

The link workers picked up cases from their assigned schools by referrals managed through the head teacher or the SEN coordinator. Referrals were also made by other agencies, for example health visitors, behaviour support teachers and directly from parents themselves. Most link workers offered 'drop in' facilities for parents, either through a formal base such as the local children's centre or through regular availability in school, such as one afternoon a week at the end of the school day.

How effective are the home school community link workers?

Of the 17 detailed case reviews, all showed positive outcomes from the perspective of the schools and the families involved. An overview of five representative case studies is shown in Table 4.1, including direct quotes from schools and carers.

The perspectives of schools and other services

Of the 19 schools sampled (17 primary and 2 secondary), 18 of the schools represented felt very positively about the service provided by the link workers. They noted a number of features of the role in constructing this positive view:

- the personal qualities of the individual link workers;
- the value of informal referral;
- the reduction in pressure and anxiety for heads and SEN coordinators;
- the quality of the information received, completing the picture and allowing schools to have more choices as to possible ways forward with children – and usually enabling them to take a more generous line than they might have done without the 'richer' information;
- making a difference for families;
- continuity and the bridging of gaps with other agencies.

The comments below are typical of responses from schools across the pilots:

... she is committed and reliable ... tenacious at making contact with families ...

(SEN coordinator)

Table 4.1 An overview of the effectiveness of home school community link workers in five representative case studies

	Reason for referral	Support for carer	Support for child	Outcomes: school perspective	Outcomes: carers perspective	Outcomes: current status
1	Self-referral. Mother anxious about child and the process of seeking specialist support.	Weekly talks with mother, re. child's problems; support through referral processes, including going with parents to meetings with specialists; support with diagnosis of Asperger's; support with behaviour management for both child and a younger sibling.	Feedback to school re. child's problems and negotiated with school to ensure additional support in a nurturing group. Child troubled by the lunchtime sessions in the big hall and so spends this time in the link worker's (LW's) lunchtime group.	'We are all now working really well together. His learning has really improved over the last year.' He no longer needs the nurturing group and now only uses the lunchtime respite.	'She sees my son at school and ensures the person he really likes pops in to see him every day, but I think she is most helpful to me ... She comes to see me and gives me a chance to unload ... I couldn't have got through without her.'	LW seeing mother regularly 1:1 for two years but now lighter touch with mother who is much calmer and now coming to courses at the children's centre.
2	Self-referral, following divorce and as a result of mother feeling she couldn't cope.	1:1 support; introduction to courses at the children's centre.	Both children came on the farm project for a week, which was run by the LW in the summer holidays.	N/A	'It has helped us a lot ... really benefited us as a family ... the children's behaviour has improved, she has really helped me with that ... I wouldn't have been able to hold down work without her ...'	Contact now through the children's centre ... 'Her number is always there if I need her, nice to feel you are not just written off ...'
3	Referral from school re.	1:1 support for mother; support with negotiations	N/A	Child has been very successful in school	'She wrote to the council for me about	Mother no longer needing support.

depressed mother, poor housing and child intimidated by neighbours and linked to this, child unhappy, not sleeping and poor attendance.	at the housing department; and classes at the children's centre.		this year, he is settled and he is working hard and has good attendance at school. He now represents his class on the school council.	getting the tiles fixed to stop the damp and to get rehoused to get away from the neighbour ... we have moved and that is fine now ... I've been back to school as well, and met friends.'	Now playing a significant role in a parents' group that supports the children's centre.
4 Referral from school following the break-up of parents' marriage and financial worries from husband's gambling debts.	Support for mother, re. behaviour management strategies with the children; treatment for depression; getting youngest child into nursery early; getting the oldest child into the secondary school she wanted to go to; negotiating with bailiffs; helping husband with accommodation nearby.	Set up a mentor for the oldest child to ease the transition into secondary school.	'She has really supported the family in a very positive way and I know they have felt they have benefited from that' (Headteacher). 'Oldest daughter settled in well following mentor relationship' (EP).	'She has done a brilliant job propping me up ... she helped me sort out my problems and helped B ... [husband] to find somewhere else near to live so he could continue to support me with the kids ...'	Mother a very competent financial manager now she has charge of the finances, so family finances now sorted. LW continues light touch contact.
5 Referral from school re. child with a statement for behaviour problems,	Support for mother re. getting rehoused. Other agencies involved. Referred to Child and Adolescent Mental Health	Support in an activity and social skills group.	'LW came to school meetings with the boy and mum and she helped mum rehearse what she	'My son was always being labelled "bad", which upset me ... it was great having someone who	Ongoing support through children's centre contact. 'I don't need her as

Table 4.1 (contd)

Reason for referral	Support for carer	Support for child	Outcomes: school perspective	Outcomes: carers perspective	Outcomes: current status
following exclusion from first primary school. Single mother with 3 children living in a refuge.	Services (CAMHS) in year 6 and LW supported her in getting to CAMHS appointments. Support with behaviour management strategies for children and help linking into mental health networks and the children's centre.		wanted to say, this made the meetings a lot less stressful for everyone and the situation has really moved forward now. He has improved from a low starting point and now much more confident and recently taken off his PSB.'	understood, and could give emotional support and offer choices and options. She comes to the school meetings with me and helps me to understand their point of view and helps me to meet them in the middle.'	much now because I have got myself sorted out and gone back to college, but I know I can contact her any time if I need her.'

... referral is very casual ... I can respond to need immediately and without getting bogged down by forms, thresholds and waiting lists ...

(Head teacher)

... she has been a fantastic support ... I have seen her as a preventative measure before things get too difficult ...

(Head teacher)

... she helps parents to process review meetings especially if the children have behaviour problems, when it works well there is a really good rapport and that helps parents, some of these meetings are very hard for the parents and to have a sympathetic independent person is really supportive for them ...

(SEN coordinator)

... although you can meet with parents in school and in the children's centre, you can't necessarily give them the 'in house' time that enables someone to relax and say I am struggling, and it is someone who can come back next week and the week after until something kicks in, the other thing is that things can go well for a while and then they need your help again ... and the link worker is still there ...

(Head teacher)

... they [link workers] are the glue that keeps the whole system together

(Head teacher)

Members of other services raised many of the same issues as head teachers as to the value of the service, but a particular feature of this feedback was the amount of collaborative work that had developed in a very short space of time:

I think it is one of the most valuable resources available to me because of the nature of the children I work with, and the amount I have to do, I always feel very frustrated that I can't do as much as I would like to do with parents ... I still go in and do initial visits but if there is any further support needed I refer back to the school and use the link worker ...

(Behaviour support teacher)

The perspectives of parents

All of the 20 parents interviewed were very positive about the contribution of the link workers to their lives. The questionnaire data were also entirely positive, but gave little information about the reasons for the positive response or about how the role might be developed, and so have not been included here.

These excerpts are taken directly from the interviews with parents (the link workers' names have been replaced with 'she' and 'her'). There were four major themes that emerged from the parents:

- qualities of the workers;
- emotional support;
- support through the process of referral to other professionals and meetings in school;
- impact on their children.

The qualities of the workers

These comments came in response to a question about how helpful they had found the link worker. All parents and carers had a positive stance in relation to this question and the qualities of warmth, care and being a good listener recurred throughout the data. However, there was also frequent reference, as in the second excerpt here, to a firmness of approach!

> She is really friendly and we have a laugh and she cheers me up if I have a problem ... other people listen to a certain extent but they don't really give you ideas and practical suggestions like she does ...

> She doesn't judge, when you are struggling she is easy to tell things to, she is very supportive but if she thinks you are getting it wrong she will tell you ... she also follows up if you cancel a meeting, one week my daughter was sick and she rang in the evening to see how I was, and she always keeps contacting you, which makes it feel very personal and reassuring – you are not just a number on a list ...

> I wouldn't be without her ... she is so good with me when I feel down and even when my son is in trouble she always says to me, I know he is a nice boy really ... he is good at heart ...

> ... She has patience, she really cares, you can trust her and you

can knock her down and she always comes back, and the children feel the same ... she quietly listens and then she puts her view to you ... she can't change the situation but she makes you feel better ... she gives of herself, when she first rang me I was a bit cynical and I thought 'another one of them', but I was so wrong ...

Emotional support

These begin with an account of one mother with a very sick child who had previously tried to access support from a social worker and health visitor but in each case had not met the criteria for involvement. The importance of spending time and 'coming alongside' are clearly illustrated here:

She has been absolutely fantastic she comes and sits on my sofa with me whilst I have a good cry ... she tells all the teachers what is going on and gets them organized to talk to each other so that I don't have to tell all the different people in the same school the same thing, and she liaised with all the other professionals involved and got them to talk to each other ... and she came to clinic appointments with me and helped with the kids so that I could actually concentrate on what the consultants were saying .... And she found I should be eligible for a higher-level disability allowance ... which has made all the difference to me. I couldn't have done it without her because I just didn't have the time, and I didn't have the emotional energy to face it all. She has been the linch pin.

The trouble is the kids control me and tell me what to do ... she got me to go to the clinic so that I could see a psychologist about my agoraphobia ... I couldn't do anything I just used to sit and cry ... she comes round every Wednesday and I feel that is time for me and I look forward to it and clean up before she comes round, she tells me I am in charge of the boys, and not them controlling me ... and now I go out and come up the children's centre ...

My son has ADHD ... and when he went to secondary school they said they couldn't have him except for a few hours a week because they couldn't cope with his behaviour and so I was just left with him and when he came home I couldn't manage his behaviour either and I thought I was going to have a nervous breakdown he was just so difficult ... I don't know what I would have done without her, she has been my rock for a long time.

Since I have been meeting with her I feel confident to go back to the Children's Centre even when she is not there. I have been to lots of her courses and they are really good, we did one called 'I'm O.K. you're O.K.' and one on coping with difficult behaviour and one on assertiveness. I also go to the park [an after school club held in the local park] with her and she does activities and they are good for the kids, and give me ideas, but also there is another adult to talk to so it is more enjoyable for me, and I can chat to her about things . . .

Support through the process of referral to other professionals and meetings in schools

These comments demonstrate the ways in which parents were being offered something, through the positioning of the link worker, that was rather different from, and provided mediation of, other services:

I am not a good talker . . . I would always end up getting angry and arguing, so she would speak for me . . .

She comes with me to the clinic . . . to see the psychologist and to meetings in school, the psychologist talks really quickly and doesn't really listen and I ask him to explain what he means but then I don't understand at the end of the session, there is so much going on in my head, so she comes with me to clarify things. When we have to go into school to explain what the psychologist has said, she comes with us and is a back-up system, she is like the minutes of the meeting recording everything that has happened . . .

She calms me down . . . I get irate and angry when I feel I am not being listened to . . . schools have a very black and white view . . . sometimes I feel very intimidated by all the people, especially if you are not expecting it . . . I went to an IEP meeting and I was taken to the head's office and there was this huge table and a dozen other adults and I felt extremely uncomfortable, and I left half way through and when I was outside I cried . . . it is so frustrating and I can't get the right words out and they are all so matter of fact and unemotional . . . and she helps me to understand their point of view and helps me to meet them in the middle . . .

Impact on their children

These perspectives are typical of the variety and detail given in response to the question, 'What difference did the link worker make for your child'? One mother's comment, 'I think it has made a difference to him because it has made a difference to me ...' was similar to those made by many respondents.

> She answers any questions I have about how to manage the children.

> She gives me ideas about what to do if they are arguing – how to manage it without telling them off, 'I' statements, wall charts and things.

> She is very firm with my son, she said 'you have two choices, you come with me to school, in my car now, or your mother will have to go to court' ... he puts his head down when he sees her but he goes ... she said 'I am not going to make excuses for you' ... it is very difficult to get him back to school after the holiday ... he won't go for me but goes if she is coming and he is better at school now ...

> I think it has made a difference to him because it has made a difference to me, and I have been more able to help him through his exclusions and things and better at dealing with the school through it all, because I know my rights. And she has got lots of things for him, through the children's fund, and has helped us get after-school clubs and school uniforms for all of them, and a holiday and she has helped me fill in forms for his DLA, which I didn't even know about, because money has been extremely tight ...

> She gives him a chance and he trusts her and when things go wrong he can talk things through with her ... and I know that is really important to him ... and really reassuring for me ...

The particular contributions of the role of the home school community link worker

What is striking about these data from parents is that many of the features that seem to be valued by parents are ones not available in other services, where it is not usually possible for parents to self refer, or if they can, to have access according to their own perception of need. Further, the support is shaped by coming alongside parents and giving them quality time at the point where it is required. A number of link workers talked about the importance of time and waiting for relationships to develop, allowing human sense to be made, and the trust that builds through small acts of practical support. The time spent, and the quality of relationship that resulted, seemed to be directly linked to the parents' perception of the effectiveness of the support. The trust that the workers managed to achieve provided a foundation for children and their families upon which they could build confidence and risk change. Over a timescale of one to two years, many of the children and family members were able to move through a stage of being quite dependent on the workers, to a point where they contacted them infrequently, having developed their own support networks, through for example, activities at the children's centre. However, even at the stage of infrequent contact parents felt they were still connected and only a phone call away from sharing new challenges or accessing further support.

The positioning of parents

As well as supporting the capacity for change through the building of trust, the ways in which the link workers operated, positioned parents as active agents in the process of support. The support was offered to them, rather than allocated to them and in many cases they had actually referred themselves. The link workers' practice was to 'come alongside', taking the agenda from the children and their carers, rather than being seen as 'fixing' externally identified problems. This changes the relationship between children and families and support, giving them more control over the relationship that ensues. The very title, 'home school community link worker', positions parents equally with the others to be linked with, and emphasizes the community as well as the school as an important context in children's lives. It also positions parents as people making choices about their own personal development rather than people being referred for remediation. It was interesting to see how parents 'normalized' their experiences, so that no parent interviewed talked about 'parenting groups' but rather about 'classes' at the children's centre or college.

This more user-led model of working is possible for the link workers because they are an emergent service. The relationship does not have to be defined by an assessment phase where the incoming professional necessarily sets the agenda according to the kind of expertise they have to offer. They do not have thresholds to satisfy or targets to meet, so they are free to maintain focus on the child and their family. Further, they have not set the kinds of professional boundaries that mean having begun a relationship they pass the relationship on to a more suitable professional or close the case. And finally, their boundaries do not preclude them from giving the support that is required, when it is required – whether this be achieving charity funding for football training, supporting families in ringing the housing office or taking the children to Matalan for new knickers.

The link workers did frequently recruit a range of professional expertise, but at the same time maintained a continuity role, fading into the background while a child had a six-week mental health intervention, but liaising with the specialist worker and being around at the end of the period to ensure the benefits of the intervention were maintained. Through their joint working, they were often able to help parents process the specialist support they were receiving, and keep communication going, so that schools were able to respond in a supportive way to the extra pressures a therapeutic intervention might bring.

An independent role

Link workers were also viewed by parents as independent, sometimes introduced by the school but not of the school, sometimes working alongside social workers or attendance officers involved in statutory work, but mediating the process for the parents rather than instigating it. There was evidence that this mediation role allowed parents to have more voice in decision making with regard to their children with schools and services, 'hearing' parents concerns more clearly. Similarly the better quality information about children's lives allowed schools to behave more generously in their response towards them, and for parents to have a better understanding of the school's point of view.

However, this independence was sometimes problematic because it left the link workers standing slightly aside from the other services when their work left them vulnerable, raising questions about who should be supervising them, where they should actually go for support and where they are placed in the whole system of support for children. This was notably more problematic in some areas than others, depending on the maturity of the local multiprofessional system in which they were operating.

The nature of the 'intervention'

What we can see from the role of the link workers is that their intervention is not a single tightly designed event that can be easily measured. For example in case study 1 (see Table 4.1), it is impossible to say whether things are going better because of the short informal daily contact from somebody the child is close to; or that the mother is less anxious because she has someone to offload on to; or that everyone's improved interactional skills mean family relationships are less fractious; or that the monthly visit for counselling is resolving underlying mental health issues; or that the link worker's taxiing the family to the counselling appointment and talking through the session is giving children access to mental health services that were 'lost in translation' before. And in case study 3, it is hard to judge whether the child is now flourishing at school because he is not living in a damp house with next-door neighbours that terrify him; or because his attendance has been closely monitored and supported; or that his mother is now less depressed, getting out and achieving new goals at college. The likelihood is that it is a subtle accumulation of all these changes that builds confidence and resilience for both the children and their parents, and that the support needs to be sustained to consolidate these small changes until families are able to draw confidently on universal services.

Continuity and overview

The link workers were in a good position to see the whole system of relationships in which the carer and child were embedded, and to help them take control of that system to better meet their needs. They were able to amplify the voice of children and their parents so that their perspectives can better influence their environment and the decisions that are being made about their lives, and attenuate some of the patterns of behaviour that were diminishing those opportunities. In short, they were 'minding' the system of relationships around the child, creating a bubble of safety where change could take place. Interestingly this continuity was a feature of other types of early intervention. Another Children's Fund evaluation designed to intervene early to reduce offending behaviour in children under 13 (Glenny 2007b) involved youth workers in a similar role, providing complex packages of support and ensuring everybody was kept in the communication loop, to amplify the feedback for the child when they were able to make small steps forward. In doing this, they were using the same skills, and acting in the same way as the system minder was managing the multiprofessional forums discussed in Chapter 3. The value of this role has also been picked up in a number of other studies, for example the role of the 'support workers' described by Webb and Vulliamy (2004). The system minding role seems to recur at the different levels in which systems emerge, or can be bounded. Like fractal structures, the larger patterns are made from multiple examples of smaller patterns of similar type: what is known in complexity science, as *nested systems*. This will be more fully discussed in the next chapter.

Thus the role of the link worker is an example of the way in which an 'appreciative system' allows the support services to customize their provision to meet local need. However, as in the case of the link workers, the local need driven response in one area also seemed to be a need in other areas, allowing the Children's Fund to give coordination and direction to the setting up of this kind of provision across a number of localities.

What was interesting in looking at these data was the huge difference in quality between the questionnaire and interview data collected. The questionnaires gave a picture of global success or failure of the services but gave very little data to inform service design or change. The individual and group sessions on the other hand provided a rich source of detail that informed and challenged the multiprofessional practice taking place in the area, providing invaluable feedback to the local forum, not just on individual services but crucially on the way the services interacted together.

We turn next to consideration of how services can interact more effectively to achieve a positive problem solving culture, promoting services that are responsive to the diversity of need in their particular area.

5 Achieving a positive problem solving culture

Emergence of new services

A group of senior social workers at a conference, listening to the evaluation findings on the role of the link workers discussed in the previous chapter, were wistfully discussing how the activities the link workers were involved in, used to be their role. Other discussions at the conference centred on the potential vulnerability of the workers and their training needs, and again there was discussion about not 'reinventing the wheel' for social work mark two. Pressure on social work resources has meant that thresholds for social work involvement have become higher and higher so that the role of the majority of social workers, within children's services, has now become an extension of the criminal justice system, largely taken up by child protection and youth offending concerns. Meanwhile the role they used to play is a gap in provision that has become noticeable enough to galvanize the development of new services. And these services have not just emerged in one local authority but very similar roles have been the focus for bids for monies from the Children's Fund, across the UK.

The *Every Child Matters* (DfES 2004) agenda sets out a framework that implies a much broader community and welfare role for schools than has been the case in the recent past, so, as one social worker noted, 'they seem to want more social work, but not done by social workers'! At the same time, many schools, having sharpened the focus of their resources to maximize educational attainment to respond to the standards debate, are not anxious to have their energies 'dissipated' by what they see to be new responsibilities.

Managing dilemmas and constraints

The dilemma about who will do the social work, and indeed what social work will be carried out, is an example of the conflicting constraints that beset children's services. These constraints are generated by the tensions around the choices made in the allocation of resources, and the professional judgements that determine the application of those resources. Whatever system is set up these dilemmas remain, but what emerged from the evaluations in Chapter 2 was that the 'successful' multiprofessional communication systems specifically addressed, and indeed mapped, the *upstream* and *downstream* provision.

We have adopted the terms 'upstream' and 'downstream' work, because the emphasis on continuity helps avoid the often rather artificial polarization of the early intervention versus threshold/crisis intervention discussion. Thus multiprofessional conversations need to mediate:

- ways of organizing professional engagement around children in difficulties (downstream solutions); with
- means of involving agencies in a wider agenda around creating environments in which fewer children have difficulties (upstream solutions).

The upstream–downstream dimension allows a wider consideration of how the whole stream could be managed and what good upstream, midstream and downstream work might mean. It includes the role of universal services and in so doing, broadens thinking about the nature of 'upstream interventions' and the relationship between universal services and specialist provision (see Figure 5.5).

The issues raised by the discussion of, 'Who is doing the social work?' are illustrative of the need to map provision in terms of the upstream–downstream dimension. How is it that the management of services is such that they can migrate downstream? At the same time, why is there a tendency for services to proliferate rather than current services adapting to meet developing areas of need? What seems to be happening is that services are perceived as unresponsive and as a result new services are created to meet the need. In the case of our example, social services has 'gone downstream' leaving a gap which has to be filled by a new set of people. One of the features of a new service is that it is malleable, the tensions of trying to deal with older services 'who won't play', can be avoided, gone round. The service can be shaped by the people who find the money, and can be shaped to fit the perceived gaps in provision. However, the result can be services growing haphazardly, resulting in more liaison time and more coordination difficulties, exacerbating the culture that encourages services to define their own terms of engagement and behave as autonomous entities. And as a further consequence, the knowledge held by the longstanding services is not fully utilized and another group of people re-invent the wheel. By avoiding the tensions, and therefore the dialogue, the contributions of the old knowledge are lost.

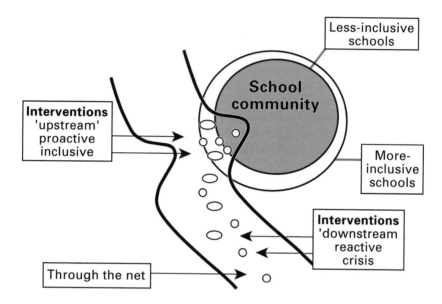

Figure 5.5 The timing of interventions: 'upstream–downstream'

Although the dilemmas that require the mapping of upstream and downstream provision are many and various, the evidence from our studies suggests that they can be clustered into a small number of key questions:

- What is the appropriate balance between upstream and downstream work?
- How is the transition managed between universal and specialist services?
- To what extent should resources be shared between working with children and working with their families?
- How do we enable service users to shape local services?

What is the balance between upstream and downstream work?

Many of the children at the upstream stage will be downstream at a later point in time, but the underlying rule is that the resources are allocated to those in greatest need, thus children are left to become 'worst cases' in order for these resources to be allocated fairly. However, this 'fair' allocation model changes over time as resources for particular services ebb and flow. What constitutes a worst case is determined by the particular capacity of a particular service at a given moment in time, for example in the migration of the role of social workers previously discussed. Thus children do not receive interventions at the optimum time but at a time regulated by a particular pattern of service provision. So what constitutes an optimum time for intervention? Common-sense would suggest that intervening early would be beneficial both in having less of a problem to resolve and in producing less damage to the context in which a child, young person or their family is embedded. However, there are limitations to this argument. First, problems presented by many pupils are temporary, and clear up without specialist support. Second, some conditions (for example, just over half the pupils assessed as displaying signs of psychiatric disorder in one study) present problems for the first time in adolescence (Rutter and Madge 1976). On the other hand there is a substantial body of research, that provides evidence that vulnerability increases with the accumulation of risk factors, and that these build over time (for example, Prior and Paris 2005). Thus the reduction of risk factors at the earliest stage should result in a reduced vulnerability to potential problems.

Prior and Paris (2005) and others (for example Galloway and Goodwin 1987) have drawn attention to the difficulties some children have with relationships as a major causative factor in later emotional and behavioural problems. In these cases, the eventual presenting problem is secondary to the child's central needs and concerns, usually identified much earlier. Further, some children's needs are severe for them, but do not reach levels of concern that result in support kicking in, particularly if they go about their problem quietly. This was illustrated by a young man on a communication skills course, who described how what he had learnt had made a huge difference to his life, a life previously blighted by relationship problems and suicidal feelings. However, his access to the course was fortuitous: he had only gained a place to make up the numbers for a group running for a number of 'targeted' children (Glenny 2007b).

Prior and Paris also draw attention to a large body of research showing that the deterioration in family contexts and disengagement with school, present significant risk factors, and again these build gradually over time. This evidence for the prevalence of multifactorial causes for vulnerability demonstrates the way in which children exist in their own system of relationships, subject to the same issues of complex interdependence, emergence, amplification and attenuation as the multiprofessional services that support them (discussed in Chapter 3). These complex systems are recognized in the assessments of the many practitioners trained in social interactionist approaches and provide the main focus for therapeutic approaches such as systemic family therapy (Minuchin 1974; Dowling and Osborne 1994) and applications of the systemic approach used to explore the teacher/learner relationship (Blow 1994). However, the support systems as a whole are not always set up to operate as if this were the case. If they were, children would be allocated their own system minder, coming alongside to support their own growing intentions with respect to navigating their lives, assisting them in getting access to the specialist support that they need as they feel they need it.

Interestingly, such a role has been developed as part of the universal provision in many European countries. Known, as the 'pedagogic' approach, with quotation marks to indicate differences in the European and English use of the word, the European pedagogue: '. . . sees herself/ himself as a person in relationship with the child as a whole person (not just, for example, a child to be taught) supporting the child's overall development: physical, cognitive, social, creative . . .' (Petrie 2005: 177). However, despite the detailed research carried out by Petrie and others at the Thomas Coram Institute, and the pressing need for new models of working with children and young people presaged by the *Every Child Matters* (ECM) framework, the 'pedagogic' approach remains on the drawing board in Britain.

What the case studies we reviewed demonstrated was that children were likely to receive intermittent support from different professionals with variable amounts of coordination. At the same time, this support was likely to be allocated to them as a result of a defined category of need, identified by organizations and professionals, with little opportunity for their own analysis of their situation to be explored. With the ECM agenda, the coordination is likely to improve with the instigation of lead professionals, but as senior professionals they will not have the time for the 'coming alongside' necessary for the 'system minder role'. On the other hand, in a number of studies we have looked at, there was evidence of key workers functioning in exactly this way. The link workers discussed in the previous chapter established just such a relationship with both children and their parents, and in a separate study (Glenny 2007b) youth workers provided very effective support by starting from and staying with the young person's perspective. It is important to note, however, that the workers we saw who were very effective in these roles, were either very experienced themselves, or were closely tied into a multiprofessional support network. However, similar findings have emerged from other evaluations (for example, Webb and Vulliamy 2004). Thus the very act of balancing upstream and downstream support raises important questions about the nature of interventions and the effectiveness of support given, that can't be addressed by individual services acting alone.

How do we manage the transition between universal and specialist services?

The focus on the context, making 'upstream' as safe as possible as an environment for children, resonates with the agenda for inclusion (DfEE 1997). From a vantage point where upstream and downstream can be viewed together, it is possible to see the contributions of different universal services, for example schools and children's centres, to the flow downstream. It was clear from the case studies collected that the internal structure and processes in schools and children's centres had a significant impact on the life chances of the children and young people they served, and specifically whether, and how quickly, they were carried off downstream (see Figure 5.5).

Now, this is not a new finding: Tony Dessent documented the ways in which schools could function more inclusively more than 20 years ago (Dessent 1986) and debates about inclusion have generated a substantial and continuing discourse ever since. This is also acknowledged in the way support systems are organized around schools with, for example, educational psychologists, specialist support teachers and educational social workers all available as a resource for schools to draw upon. However, despite this rhetoric on inclusion, backed up by Ofsted inspection data (Ofsted 2000) and target setting, schools are not financially rewarded for inclusive behaviour. The speed of children's movement from upstream to downstream will be dependent on the capacity of the school, and schools who do not behave inclusively benefit from spending less of their resources on vulnerable children.

People in schools are the people most likely to notice the developmental concerns and emotional and behavioural changes that indicate vulnerability. However, many schools are not well set up to carry out the detailed case work and commitment to action that initial concerns may warrant. In our studies it was clear that some schools had given much greater attention to these issues than others, and this made a significant difference to the quality of the provision for the vulnerable children and young people in their care. At the same time, these intrinsically more inclusive schools were also more able to engage effectively with services external to the school. Thus the children were less likely to require specialist support, but if they did need it they were more likely to receive appropriate and timely intervention.

In *Every Child Matters: Change for Children* (DfES 2004), it is argued that extended schools are at the heart of the delivery of the ECM agenda with the aim to increase the number of services that are available within schools. However, apart from the expense of every school being resourced in this way, we found some evidence to suggest that this might be problematic. Link workers talked about the importance of being seen as independent from schools, particularly when they were effectively operating in a mediation role (Glenny 2007a). At the same time, schools were very clear that it was precisely the 'outsider status' of the youth workers that enabled them to start working with the young people uncontaminated by a fraught history with the school, enabling the young people to get a genuinely fresh start (Glenny 2007b).

Vulliamy and Webb (1999), evaluating a Home Office funded project placing social workers in schools, found it to be a successful way of tackling crime; nevertheless they noted unexpected problems. The social workers had been placed in the secondary school in order to provide a service to the secondary school and the feeder primaries that made up a school cluster. They found that the social worker was absorbed by the needs of the secondary school and therefore had difficulty finding time to meet the needs of the primary schools, even though the total cluster represented a smaller 'patch' than any social worker in the area had previously held. Further, the social worker was supported in sloughing off what were perceived to be the excessive demands of the primary heads by colleagues in the secondary school protecting *their* resource. Meanwhile, some of the work that the social worker was doing was very similar to that of a school counsellor in other schools. Vulliamy and Webb noted that similar findings had been reported in similar Home Office project evaluations in another part of the country.

These examples suggest that extended services, working across the kind of school partnerships evaluated in Chapter 2, may provide more opportunities for establishing a good balance between upstream and downstream solutions, and provide a better reach for all children in the community, regardless of which school they attend.

However the interface is relocated, there is always an interface that needs to be negotiated and, it follows, a need to be competent at negotiating interfaces. For this reason, managers' attempts to 'design out' the interfaces, are often surprisingly unsuccessful, as we saw in the example of the school based social worker above. Co-locating services is frequently argued to be at the heart of multiprofessional success: get everyone together over the photocopier and communication difficulties will disappear. However, the experience of child guidance clinics demonstrates that co-location is not a universal panacea. Sampson's (1980) analysis suggests that while some clinics worked very well, others worked very badly, providing a battlefield for internecine war and power politics. Anning et al. (2006: 107) found a similarly mixed picture:

> Co-location assists but does not guarantee effective joint work-
> ing. Our findings indicated there can still be problems with

communication and shared working activities within co-located settings ... one of the unintended consequences of developing joined up teams is that they can generate what we identified as 'core' and 'peripheral team members ... [and they note] ... people can feel peripheral where most of the team are co-located but some are not.

This would seem to be true across national boundaries. A recent comparative study of multiprofessional working in Sweden and the UK has data from which the authors draw similarly mixed conclusions on the value of co-location (Petrie et al. in press). There also seem to be some dangers in groups becoming over-identified with each other, for example the flawed decision making reported in Janis's (1972) classic book *Victims of Groupthink* and Hemmelgarn et al.'s (2006: 76) findings that 'organizations with particularly strong shared cultures were found to be less innovative, explained by possible resistance to change of well-established norms ...'. Co-location can also be expensive both in time, waiting for the restructuring, and in money, building the new buildings. The setting up of co-located working can provide exactly the disruption that we argue in Chapter 3, is so damaging for complex communication systems.

This is not to suggest that co-location is in itself problematic, but rather that it is unlikely to produce solutions in isolation from the consideration of the whole system of relationships in which the co-located field workers are engaged.

To what extent should resources be shared between working with children and working with their families?

One of the dilemmas for the link workers (discussed in Chapter 4) was that as their role developed they were increasingly being required to work with children's families rather than the children themselves. They frequently described having to re-timetable work with children because they needed to prioritize a crisis situation with a family. While it was certainly true that, as one parent said, 'it has made a difference to him because it has made a difference to me', what again was happening was a service drifting downstream. Warin (2007) draws attention to the conflict of goals that underlies many policy initiatives in childcare. She contests the assumed harmony suggested by policy makers between the needs of parents and children, and draws attention to the potential conflict between getting parents back into work and providing better quality experiences for their children. She calls for 'goals to be clarified and centred on the "child within the family" as the targeted beneficiary of services' (Warin 2007: 88) and concludes: 'we may need to reconceptualise the family in a child-centred way in order to provide a clearer basis for the integration of services. This clarification would ensure that children's services prioritise and act as advocates for, the needs of children' (p. 95).

How do we enable service users to shape local services?

In the studies in which we were involved, there were few robust and systematic pathways for engaging service users in the design of services. There were, however, a number of emerging practices that could provide a basis for more thoroughgoing user involvement.

The first of these was a children and young people's forum, created across a cluster of primary and secondary schools serving a county town and surrounding villages (Glenny 2005a). The forum consisted of representatives from the school council of each school, drawing on issues raised in their individual school councils. While the forum discussions focused on issues pertaining to universal provision, it would be a small step to ask the group to engage with issues raised in the multiprofessional forum. Further, the current contributions of the group often related to issues beyond the school, for example the development of community resources for young people out of school time, and thus directly feeding into discussion of 'upstream' provision.

A second series of developments centred on the local Children's Fund, through the post of a participation officer (described by Partridge 2005). The participation officer led a number of groundbreaking projects, supporting children in engaging in decision making processes at every level of the Children's Fund organization and providing a children and young people's sounding board for the local authority. This very innovative work included the allocation of £50,000 to a series of area-based 'community chests', in which the children (aged 5–13) received requests for support from other children with a range of needs, and through discussion at a panel, allocated the resources. The community chest was run entirely by the children – supported by the participation officer – from the design of the application forms to the writing and sending of the cheques.

A third approach to consultation had developed in a children's centre that was itself a local hub of multiprofessional activity, managing the area multiprofessional forum for a small group of primary and secondary schools (reported in Glenny 2005a). This children's centre had originally been set up by the local community and had maintained a community steering group, following a change from independent status to local authority control. As well as the steering group the children's centre had developed a range of approaches to informal participation and feedback to inform decision making. Through such processes they were able to draw on the views of a large percentage of the people using the centre and associated services and evaluate the range of multi-professional services for that community. And because of the close relationships with schools these data represented work with children and their families right through primary and into the secondary stage.

What all of these examples show is the potential ease with which children, young people and their carers can contribute directly to decision making processes when this is systematically managed at a local level, and particularly when someone has responsibilities and skills in facilitating participation.

Communication structures for the discussion of upstream–downstream issues

How can the configuration of children's services ensure that services remain positioned to maximize their potential for the user and at the same time draw on the knowledge and experience held by experienced field workers across disciplines? How can services provide continuity but at the same time have the capacity and flexibility to meet new challenges? How can they ensure the participation of those using the services in this ongoing design process?

Our data suggest that where participation happens successfully, discussions of all these issues take place at a point where the whole system of communication and practice can be seen interacting together. The successful multiprofessional communication systems (reported in Chapter 2) provide a space for reflection upon how services for children worked together, and in particular, on how the upstream and down-stream dilemmas could be mapped and resolved. However, as we have previously argued in Chapter 3 (p. 49), this mapping process only seemed to be successful where the levels of complexity are manageable. That is, where the performance of a particular group of professionals can be evaluated by a particular community of users and field workers who are using or observing the service. At this level, it was possible to see the whole picture so that patterns could be observed and sense could be made.

Depending on the configuration of the local areas, these spaces for making sense varied, but in all the local areas there was a communica-tion hub, where different strands of communication were brought together, what we will call here a local 'forum'.

If optimum size was one feature of the local forums, the nature of the evidence upon which they were drawing, was another. The issues brought to the forums were based on the particular cases of particular field workers. Through the personal interrogation of particular cases, individual field workers were able to identify the critical issues determining their practice. These issues (i.e., rather than the discussion of individual cases) then become the substance of the forum discussion. The forum, by encouraging field workers to think systematically about their case work, was able to capture the complexity of the people and contexts with which they were working, but at the same time pick up on patterns that persisted across examples, patterns that were frequently recognized by other field workers referring back to their own cases. Once these patterns had been drawn out, the forums were able to look at the patterns emerging over a wider sample of cases, to collect more detailed information and explore resolutions.

What was also interesting was that despite the richness of discussion that was generated by the issues drawn from individual cases, field workers seemed apologetic about their 'anecdotal' examples, the case that told a story. However, there would seem to be no such embarrassment in the legal profession about the use of case law, or in natural history about the role of local observers. To illustrate this point, for a long time before the discovery of the problems with DDT, local ornithologists were reporting that the eggs of birds of prey were found broken in their nests because the shells were so thin. Local knowledge was crucial to the construction of a picture that eventually resulted in an understanding of why these birds were not reproducing, and from this knowledge came policy change. But some birds were on the point of extinction before this happened. The timescale for damage to children cannot be so long. It is the people in the field who can see what is happening, and it is in the forums that the data are filtered and recorded. All the policy makers need to do is to ensure they have good systems to capture these rich data.

The configurations of the local forums

We have argued throughout this book that in multiprofessional work there will always be interfaces that need to be managed. The process of managing them seems to be dependent on opportunities for good quality communication between field workers. However, there did not seem to be one particular communication set-up or model that was better than others: good outcomes were achieved from a range of communication structures differently configured. Furthermore, some structures that were set up varied in effectiveness over time because although the structure looked the same, some of the initial conditions changed (for example, see p. 39). Below, we review some of the successful configurations and try to draw out what features made them effective. Successful configurations were:

- networks;
- steering groups;
- the children's centre multiprofessional hub.

Networks

One of the features of networks is their simplicity. A network can be set up at any time by anyone calling a meeting and ensuring relevant people know about the meeting and understand its purposes. The impetus for such a meeting would be likely to come from a group of practitioners recognizing a joint issue or concern that requires joint resolution. The sustainability of these meetings depends on the value a critical number of individual members place on the opportunity to meet and talk.

In our studies there were two examples of networks: one had been functioning on a regular basis (meeting five to six times a year) for 11 years, and one had been running for a year and a half. In both cases the network boundaries were defined by the geography of a school cluster, that is, a secondary school and associated feeder primary schools. In the case of the longer-running network, the mailing list included at least 60 people, although individual network meetings were typically attended by 12–20 members. Membership ranged across voluntary and statutory agencies and at any one time the meetings would be attended by the same core group of local practitioners, together with regular members who did not necessarily come every time but would turn up to engage with a particular issue under discussion which interested them. There were also occasional members who perhaps dropped into the network when they first started working in the area or in response to a particular topic of concern. The membership of the newer network had a larger regular membership of 15–25 members. The regular core membership of both groups represented the full range of disciplines and agencies in the local area, and in both cases this included a(n):

- general practitioner;
- health visitor;
- community police officer;
- social worker;
- head teacher;
- SEN coordinator;
- educational psychologist;

- educational social worker;
- children's centre head;
- youth worker from the voluntary sector;
- mental health worker from the voluntary sector;
- church minister.

Thus it could be seen that this network had particular strengths in being inclusive: anyone who wanted to could be a member, and membership was simply a matter of turning up at a network meeting. In both cases network meetings were typically of one hour duration and were held at lunchtimes in a geographically central location. In both cases there was usually a topic on which to focus, agreed at the previous meeting, and time for informal networking. The meetings were coordinated by a member of the group who was prepared to carry out the 'system minder' role (see p. 40). In these two cases, this role was played by someone from the local secondary school (the SEN coordinator and then school counsellor in one case, the head teacher in the other).

One difference between the two was that the more established network had set up a steering group to take forward issues and actions discussed and proposed at full network meetings. This meant that in addition to network functions such as getting to know about other people's roles and responsibilities, establishing informal relationships and sharing issues, the network was evolving new practices at a local level. The steering group consisted of a representative group drawn from the network. Time for this role was then negotiated and invariably achieved by discussion with line managers at a local level. Given how fraught discussion of resources can be, it was interesting that these organizational roles seemed to be easily absorbed into the job descriptions of current practitioners in the area.

The function of these networks was therefore to provide the opportunity for formal networking, amplifying the benefits of the more ad hoc informal networking that would already be taking place. In so doing, network members were able to directly address issues raised by the interfaces between their services, identify gaps in provision and agree achievable aims for improving services to children and families. The network also enabled members to come to a better understanding of each other's roles and responsibilities and, where appropriate, to challenge and influence each other's philosophies and procedures.

Steering groups

The representative local steering group differed from a network in that membership was set up to formally represent all players in a particular local area, for example with a specific representative from the primary schools, the secondary school(s), the children's centre(s), health, the range of children's services and voluntary sector workers. The group also had formal links with the partnership heads group, the local health centres, multiagency support teams, the school consultation teams and, where they existed, service user groups such as the children and young people's forum mentioned earlier. Indeed, one of the key roles for the locality forum was to discuss the issues raised by the school consultation teams. For this reason, representation was discussed in relation to the two groups to ensure economy in the use of meeting time. So, for example, the school nurses usually chose to attend the school consultation teams, while the local health visitor represented health on the forum.

The representative forum was the local hub for communication in the area and had clear lines of communication to local authority strategic groups. It had a regular chair who worked with the local system minder, to ensure the agenda was set up and taken forward. The representative forum very often set up sub-groups to carry out particular pieces of data collection to enhance future discussion, for example the setting up of a health working group to collect more detailed information about the patterns of absences in the local schools.

Thus the representative forum had a more consistent membership than the network and a more managerial function. The more informal, field-work-focused discussions that were typical of the network took place in the school consultation teams. The network, on the other hand, had a broader, larger and more inclusive membership and looser structure. It was interesting that the different types of meeting seemed to attract different personnel. Both networks regularly had GPs attending, while the representative forum struggled to recruit GPs perhaps put off by the longer meetings and the commitment to more regular attendance that the representative forum required. The network was a 'lighter structure' and had emerged in areas that were less needy, less well resourced and more geographically spread.

The children's centre multiprofessional hub

The children's centre was positioned half way between two primary schools with good links to the secondary school fed by the primary schools and making up a coherent geographical unit, serving an identifiable, high need community. Although smaller than most 'localities' it represented the most integrated, elaborated and coherent example of multiprofessional working of the six pilot projects evaluated (Glenny 2005a). The centre had originally been set up as a community initiative and retains a strong feeling of community ownership. The centre ran multiprofessional meetings to support case work in the two schools and coordinated other multiprofessional meetings to review particular issues arising in the locality. The mix of statutory funding and independent funding had enabled the centre to bid for monies to support gaps in provision. This had included running after-school clubs, employing a link worker to work across the two schools and working with the behaviour support service to develop nurturing groups within the school. They also established the centre as a base for a number of services including social workers, resulting in much better liaison with social services than was evident in other areas. Meanwhile the head of centre functioned as a very effective 'system minder' for the mini locality.

This children's centre provides a classic example of the value of locally derived, evolving structures. It also provides an example of the potential fragility of such evolving practice, vulnerable to being swept away by top-down 'one size fits all' models.

Nested systems

In these examples the communication systems were nested and at each level a communication hub was required. In the high need areas there was a multiprofessional communication system in each school (the school consultation teams) which was formally linked to a local communication hub. In the less needy areas, schools were represented through formal communication pathways to the local network from the head teacher partnerships and SEN coordinator groups and through the individual members of these groups at the network meetings.

In the six localities study (Glenny 2005a) communication links were extended to ensure the issues from the local groups were being heard at the strategic level of the local authority. This was achieved by a member of the senior management of children's services joining each of the pilot locality groups. Since the completion of our research, this communication system has been developed further. The locality forums feed information to area groups which in turn are represented at local authority level. Thus, in principle at least, local authority decision making was informed by a rich source of data from the field.

All the multiprofessional communication systems we saw working effectively had at their heart the interface with universal service provision. This meant that schools and children's centres were not taken as a given but were as much the subject of evolutionary change as the services that worked from and around them. Our findings suggested that when they felt properly supported, schools valued the challenge of the external perspective: it was precisely in negotiating the interfaces that they were becoming more inclusive.

This seemed to be because the dominant discourse of the various forums was positive and problem solving in orientation. This allowed for the specific discussion of tensions and difficulties, rather than, as we had seen in the less successful contexts, avoidance of difficulty and the development of alternative provision and parallel working. Interestingly, the innovations developed by the urban and rural areas discussed in Chapter 2 were predominantly upstream initiatives. The gaps in provision were largely perceived to be around earlier intervention and the development of an extension to universal provision – an expansion of the educational gateway for young people. Thus projects involved working with teachers, teaching assistants and parents to help them manage behaviour better; setting up study groups to ensure inclusive solutions for children with emotional and behavioural problems; having quiet places to go in school where children could choose to take time out from the classroom if they were feeling upset or angry; having link workers available to have early conversations with children, parents or schools when indicators suggested problems might be developing.

Schools and children's centres are expected to work with other agencies both to prevent social exclusion taking place and to help reintegrate into mainstream society those who have been socially excluded. They therefore have to be at the heart of the multiprofessional endeavour. The local forums therefore need to sit astride 'upstream and downstream' interventions and ensure they are not just a multiprofessional team circling around and providing a service to the separate institutions of schools.

In whatever way these forums are structured, their function was to configure the environment in which everyone was working to provide the best possible support for the children and young people in their care. In order to do this there was a continual evolution of practice at the interfaces between services, between schools and communities, between individual practitioners, such that new and creative contexts and practices evolved. Supported by outside agencies, schools were able to refresh their approaches. Examples were:

- helping the transition from primary to secondary school by training and providing support materials developed for form tutors in year 7;
- supporting vulnerable young people at lunchtimes, when they were identified as getting into difficulties, by link workers providing support groups or youth workers opening up youth club type facilities;

- the joint work between speech and language therapists and reception teachers to support children coming into school with poor language skills;
- the development of on-site health provision for young people in rural secondary schools;
- the invitations to housing officers and health visitors to deliver services and clinics within the children's centres;
- the development of the school curriculum through teachers working alongside youth workers on social skills projects and alternative curriculum opportunities;
- the continual regeneration of ideas needed to ensure that the behaviour support base remains a positive environment and doesn't degenerate into the 'sin bin'.

Through these different means, when the forums were working effectively, field workers were able to meet together in a context that facilitated the sharing of ideas, reflection and joint problem solving. Conversely, without these forums or when the forums were working in such a way as to result in 'collaborative inertia', relationships in the field were frequently fraught. In the next chapter we explore some of the dynamics of these relationships.

6 The importance of relationships in the field

The purpose of the multiprofessional communication systems that make up the central focus of this book is to ensure: first, that universal services are supported in evolving towards providing the richest possible contexts in which children and young people can develop, defined currently by *Every Child Matters*'s five outcomes for children; second, that children who need additional help achieve the best possible support in the best possible way. Both endeavours are crucially dependent on the quality of relationships between field workers, and between field workers and the children and their carers who are using the services. In reviewing the work of the link workers in Chapter 4, we were struck by the fact that the defining feature of their work was the way in which they were achieving these relationships, not only with respect to children and families but also with schools and other field workers. The importance of relationship skills was also identified by Lindsay et al. (2007) in their much larger sample for the evaluation of the government's 'parental support advisers' initiative. This success is in contrast to our findings of an undercurrent of dissatisfaction from some parents and carers with respect to their experience of schools and other support services, for example: '... she gives of herself, when she first rang me I was a bit cynical and I thought "another one of them", but I was so wrong ...' (Glenny 2007a: 10).

So what is the problem?

As human beings we continuously negotiate the different perspectives of our friends and colleagues, we continually seek to understand what they are trying to say and do. And yet in multiprofessional contexts misunderstanding seems to be endemic and it is argued that this should be expected – how can it be otherwise with our different training and our different cultures, our different 'tribes and territories' (Becher 1989). Yet these do not seem to be sufficient reasons for difficulty. Tribes with their territories have good reason for tension because their survival may depend upon it, while field workers in children's services have a common cause: to improve conditions for children and their families. They are also likely to have strong commitments to their work, often in receipt of salaries that they could improve in other occupations. So what is it about the nature of the work that can result in poor experiences for children and families, and a subsequent focus on the differences rather than the similarities when working together?

In this chapter, we explore themes that emerged from our research that seemed to impact significantly on the quality of relationships in the field. These focused upon:

- underlying differences in values and purposes that need to be explored in order for trust to be established;
- the organization, regulation and measurement of services: interruptions to intra- and interpersonal processes for developing the understandings that underpin action;
- linking individual relationships and community responsibility: providing a context in which mutual trust and commitment can develop.

Underlying differences in values and purposes: establishing trust

Despite the apparently common agenda, and the rhetoric around collaborative working, the case studies we reviewed demonstrated that a lot of interagency collaboration is not about *collaborative activity* as such, but communicating effectively about *individual areas of work*, ensuring that the patchwork of *individual effort* in relation to a particular family made sense. Therefore the effectiveness of the individual work was crucially dependent on the quality of the communication system. Because of the individual nature of much of the work, individuals can carry out their bit of the patchwork with limited communication with other professionals. Indeed, the debates about their practice tend to focus on the nature of their own professional contribution, through discipline-based journals and discipline-based conferences, rather than the relationship of that contribution to the work of professionals in other disciplines.

In our evaluations we were often struck by the quality of the individual work we observed from field workers, even when this work did not necessarily contribute to good outcomes for children (see, for example, the case study later in this chapter, p. 101). Where communication was poor, field workers could go home at the end of the day feeling that they had done their intervention with integrity, even if subsequently things hadn't worked out for a child. Often an intervention was described as a 'good piece of work', clearly bounded by the field worker's own role. In so doing, they were likely to conclude that, first, they could do no more and, second, the failure must lie elsewhere. As we have already discussed in Chapter 1, this was usually expressed as, 'the system isn't working'.

We have already discussed the importance of practice being embedded in effective communication systems in Chapter 3. However, there is still a need to understand why individuals, wanting to make sense together, often fail to do so. In our investigations we found differences both in the underlying values held by practitioners and in how these values were emerging as purposes in relation to:

- interpretations of the same joint activity;
- the positioning of parents;
- the positioning of children;
- opportunities for dialogue and the building of trust.

Interpretations of the same joint activity

Tett et al. (2001), in an exploration of collaborative practice in schools, draw attention to underlying differences in value systems that can be masked by joint activity. They give examples of two schools running two very similar projects for vulnerable young people who had social, emotional or behavioural difficulties and would benefit from individual or small group work with support from an 'expert' from an agency outside the school.

Although both schools were offered the same resource, in one case the school selected children who were disruptive and invited the outside worker to withdraw them for individual programmes. In the other case the school selected children with a range of social, emotional and behavioural issues and paired the outside worker with a teacher to work with the children in a group. In both cases there was a desire to improve overall educational outcomes for the young people. In the first school this was seen as being most effectively achieved by working with a small number of troubled young people separately, thus enabling the school to go on working as usual. By contrast, in the second school the skills of the outsider were being taken on by a teacher within the school and approaches to group work were being developed so that the intervention could have an impact on the way the school operated in the future. Through discussion with all those involved, Tett et al. (2001) identify that superficially similar interventions actually had rather different

Table 6.1 A summary of how similar interventions had different meanings in two schools

	School 1	School 2
Values	Social and academic education for all	Academic education for the majority
Purposes	Involving young people in decision making	Minimizing the effect of problematic behaviour
Tasks	Developing all pupils socially and academically	Subcontracting out difficult pupils
Conditions	Collaborative sharing of expertise	Complementarity of expertise

meanings for the two schools on four dimensions of practice, that of values, purposes, tasks and conditions. These are summarized below (Tett et al. 2001: 19).

The example in Table 6.1 shows that any apparent common endeavour, or what Tett has described as 'task', may be underpinned by very different values and purposes, taking place in a variety of conditions. In addition, the ways and means to approach the task, even where values and purposes are shared, may vary according to the disciplinary training that a given practitioner has received. An example of this can be seen in a study of multiprofessional decision making concerning children with language difficulties (Glenny and Lown 1987). In this study, there was tension between educational psychologists and speech and language therapists who were involved in giving advice on special school placement for children with language difficulties. The tension was generated by the different understandings of the ways to support language difficulties generated by their different training experiences. Following up on 12 case studies, the professionals who were involved showed great consistency with the rest of their professional group in their constructs about language difficulty. However, the two professional groups showed differences between them in the weight they put on aspects of the children's difficulties, with very different implications for how the children should be supported. These consistent differences are shown in Table 6.2.

These differences were so evident that two of the parents interviewed remarked on the discrepancy of view and one father noted that if the professionals could not make up their minds, then their own views were as good as anyone's. However, as positive as this might have been for that particular parent, there must be cheaper ways of achieving such empowerment.

Table 6.2 A summary of differences in constructs about language difficulty between a speech and language therapist, and an educational psychologist

Speech and language therapist	Educational psychologist
Early referral, problems are cumulative so intervention should take place as soon as possible.	*Early referral suspect* because many difficulties spontaneously resolve and many children, identified early, don't go on to have difficulties.
Treat, usually with specifically targeted group or 1:1 support.	*Monitor/change context*, ensuring children have good access to a variety of rich language environments so that natural learning processes can be facilitated.
Structured approach based on a detailed analysis of the child's language.	*Setting up contexts for purposeful communication in a good language environment.*
Special placement, to achieve a stress-free environment with good adult/child ratio and specialist support.	*Local school*, focused support in a normal language environment with the developmentally appropriate models of the other children.
'Medical model' focus on deficits/language needs.	*Interactive model* needs of the 'whole child'.

This led us to look at whether the professionals across the 12 cases had agreed on the placement decisions, whether they had agreed to differ or whether they had felt their advice had not been followed in the eventual decision to place the child in the language unit. In two cases, the placement had taken place with the full agreement of both professionals and in each case it had been the same pair of professionals that had been involved. Following up on these cases, we supposed that the constructs of the speech and language therapist and the educational psychologist were not typical of their professional group, perhaps they held constructs closer to each other than was the norm. To our surprise we did not find this to be the case, they were both absolutely typical of their professional group in the constructs they held about language. However, it was clear from the children's files that they had been in discussion about the children for a longer period of time before the placement than was typical in the sample as a whole. Further investigation showed that they were friends and regularly met for lunch to share cases, thus the earlier discussion of cases was accompanied by better quality time for that discussion to take place. They recognized the differences in perspective they both had, but found this a productive challenge to their own thinking.

Following up on the other nine cases, there were varying degrees of disagreement, accompanied by a history of professional discomfort in all cases. Unlike, the resolved cases discussed above, referrals were being made to the other practitioner at a late stage in the process when each individual was already clear about what they felt the decision should be. In consequence, the eventual discussion was characterized by disagreement. The referrals were made because a joint report was a necessary part of the process rather than because there was any expectation that an interdisciplinary conversation would be helpful. The practitioners were clear that they often put off contact with the other person because of the previous history of disagreements in discussions about children. Thus a history of difficulties in a relationship led to the next interaction being in conditions most likely to lead to a fraught interaction, thus building on the relationship difficulties. What was particularly striking was the commitment of all the professionals to the making of the right decision for the children. These were not lazy or feckless people who couldn't be bothered to make the effort to achieve joint decision making, rather they were working in communication contexts that were not conducive to good quality interaction, and when failed relationships resulted there were no checks on the system to focus attention on problems or to bring about resolution.

The positioning of parents

In our studies we found differences of understanding between field workers about their roles and aims in relation to parents and the extent to which those aims related to the school and the wider community. For example, some link workers and their managers were keen to direct attention to the community aspect of the full 'home school community link worker' designation. This was often dropped by people focusing on the school context, but regarded as essential by others who saw the linking of isolated families into the community as crucial to the child's well-being. Indeed these workers frequently identified the summer holidays as a time of particular vulnerability for children.

Parents and children were also being supported quite differently in terms of the power dimensions of the relationships. For example, the title 'link worker' is relatively neutral in power terms: 'the support was offered to them, rather than allocated to them and in many cases they had actually referred themselves' (Glenny 2007a: 22). However, the government's latest pilot project for a similar kind of field worker has titled them 'parental advisers' and this positions them rather differently. While the title 'link worker' suggests a two-way interaction, the title 'parental adviser' (PA) suggests a flow of information and need for change in one direction. The interim findings from the pilot evaluation (Lindsay et al. 2007) suggest a more school-based, school-driven flavour to the work than in the role we reviewed. This perhaps reflects the government's finely balanced agenda for this initiative. As a minister summed up:

> We all need to work hard to engage parents. But in doing that we also have the right to expect and demand that parents take their responsibilities seriously too ...
>
> Delivering parental responsibility is at the heart of our education reforms – support for those parents who have not traditionally engaged with education, or need extra help in meeting their responsibilities, as well as sanctions for those that simply will not ...
>
> (Jacqui Smith, DfES 2006b)

While these seem to be fair sentiments, a slight balance towards the first or second part of each sentence can deliver a very different role. Parents themselves are very sensitive to these nuances of meaning and the positioning they imply, for example, none of the 20 parents interviewed talked about going to parenting classes, instead they had been to 'classes at the children's centre' or 'classes at college' (Glenny 2007a: 23).

Partnership with parents has been enshrined in educational policy since the White Paper *Better Schools* (DES 1985). In 1998 this was formalized with the notion of home school contracts (*Excellence in Cities*, DfEE 1998). However, a number of commentators have questioned how equal this partnership really is. Edwards (2002) argues that: 'The soft language of partnership is becoming a more hard edged attempt to direct and regulate family and home life for both parents and children' (p. 4). Similarly, Crozier and Reay (2005) have warned against the increasing pressures of aspects of school life, for example homework, as 'the colonisation of the home by the school' (p. xiii).

Moss and Petrie (2002), in an analysis of recent government policy papers, note that: 'Over and above the requirement to attend, children are increasingly subject to the gaze and agenda of the school in other ways' (p. 98). They argue that policy encourages the school to have increasing control of the use of children's time at home and to put increasing pressure on parents to fulfil managerial responsibilities with regard to children's education, through the monitoring of homework and the linking of 'out of school' activities to the schools goals. Similarly, their analysis of the papers relating to the *Early Years* shows the extension of the reach of the school into the period before compulsory attendance, in order to prepare the child for compulsory education. They conclude that these guidelines: '... purposefully extend the school's domain beyond its physical boundaries and timetable ... all of the documents we have considered speak, in short, of the growing imperium of the school and the structures of formal education' (p. 98).

Further, the notion of partnership assumes children's and their parents' interests and concerns concur. We have already referred to Warin's (2007) work on the extent to which practitioners focus on the family or the 'child within the family'. Alldred et al. (2002), investigating young people's perspectives on home school partnerships, have found some young people are not happy that parents know about their school life and vice versa, so that the young people were not universally in favour of closer links between home and school.

The positioning of children

We also observed conflicts about what field workers were hoping to achieve with children both within and beyond the educational context. Prout (2000: 304) expresses this tension in the construction of childhood very clearly:

> When it comes to children, I suggest, control and self-realisation are both present but in tension. On the one hand, there is the increasing tendency to see children as individuals with a capacity for self-realisation and, within the limits of social interdependency, autonomous action; on the other, there are practices directed at greater surveillance, control and regulation of children.

These tensions between field workers are mirrored in different aspects of government policy. *Youth Matters* (DfES 2005, 2: 12) considered four challenges which its proposals were designed to address in order to help all teenagers achieve the ECM outcomes. These were:

1   How to engage more young people in positive activities and empower them to shape the services they receive.
2   How to encourage more young people to volunteer and become involved in their communities.
3   How to provide better information, advice and guidance to young people to help them make informed choices about their lives.

4   How to provide better and more personalized intensive support for each young person who has serious problems or gets into trouble.

While these are valid questions supporting what has become a welcome shift in government's construction of childhood, there were aspects of the Green Paper clearly demonstrating the tension described by Prout (2000) between the ideas of control and self-realization. For example, the section on 'empowering young people' introduces the idea of the 'opportunity card', which will provide discounts on a range of 'things to do and places to go'. However, the section continues: 'This subsidy would be withheld from young people engaging in unacceptable and anti-social behaviours and the card suspended or withdrawn' (DfES 2005, 3: 16). Far from being a universal offer this is conditional, regulatory and discriminatory. Furthermore, it is a market orientated solution likely to result in uneven quality and provision across the country.

Moss and Petrie (2002) argue that many images of childhood take something away from children, positioning them as 'passive', 'needy' and 'weak', which they contrast with the view of Loris Malaguzzi (1993), the first head of the early childhood provision in Reggio, who wrote that 'our image of the child is rich in potential, strong, powerful and competent and, most of all, connected to adults and other children (p. 10). Gilligan (1982) develops this focus on connectedness. She critiques the priority sometimes given to developing 'autonomy' by arguing that in a caring society it is crucial also to develop 'interdependency'.

All of these constructions of childhood bump along together, underpinning practice, often in contradiction, but rarely fully explored.

Opportunities for dialogue and the building of trust

One of the features of the study of speech and language therapists and psychologists mentioned earlier was that the differences were not perceived to be a barrier, indeed were seen to be stimulating, if the opportunities for good quality dialogue were available. While it is not possible to draw any conclusions from this very small study, some aspects of the patterns observed did correspond to findings in the locality-based studies. In particular, we found that when the communication systems were going well we did not pick up evidence of the tensions between professionals of different disciplines that were very evident in the contexts where the communication systems were problematic. Most significantly, this was true even in the urban study where the personnel were the same people who had been interviewed 18 months earlier.

When professionals have good relationships, they are more likely to make the space and time to have the quality dialogue that allows them to bring their different expertise to the table. Similarly, when field workers have opportunities for quality dialogue the relationships are more likely to be good. Huxham and Vangen (2005: 154) argue that the building of trust in relationships is crucial to this understanding of the relationship being 'good'. Thus:

> ... trust building must be a cyclic process within which positive outcomes form the basis for trust development. With each consecutive positive outcome trust builds upon itself incrementally over time, in a virtuous circle. Each time partners act together, they take a risk and form expectations about the intended outcomes and the way others will contribute to achieving it. Each time an outcome meets expectations, trusting attitudes are reinforced. The outcome becomes part of the history of the relationship so increasing the chance that partners will have positive expectations about joint actions in the future ...

Anning et al. (2006) also found that joint client focused activities provided powerful opportunities for developing shared understandings. Huxham and Vangen refine the nature of these activities further in that they argue that small-scale, low-risk activities are much more likely to meet mutual expectations, so that, 'there is a strong case for initiating collaboration through modest, low risk initiatives ...' (Huxham and Vangen 2005: 154).

Huxham and Vangen also note how vulnerable such trust cycles are to unequal power relations and the perceived need of partner organizations to protect their own interests through the manipulation and control of collaborative agendas. Again we see why, with apologies to Schumacher (1974), 'smallish is beautiful'. The local communication systems were able to produce environments where these kinds of trust cycles were starting to thrive, away from the necessarily more complex and politically weighted agendas of service managers.

The implications of this are not just that the foundations of trust building are to actively engage with others in small projects, but also that the whole process of trust building takes time. As Sennett (1998: 24) observes:

> 'No long term' is a principle which corrodes trust, loyalty and mutual commitment. Trust can be a purely formal matter, as

when people agree on a business deal or rely on another to observe the rules of the game. But usually deeper experiences of trust are informal, as when people learn on whom they can rely when they are given a difficult or impossible task. Social bonds take time to develop, slowly rooting into the cracks and crevices of institutions. The short time frame of modern institutions limits the ripening of informal trust ...

This draws attention to the reasons why restructuring can be so damaging. Years of this crucial informal trust can we swept away, without any understanding of the damage that has been done. Interestingly, Sennett (1998), drawing on data from examples of organizational re-engineering in the 1990s, found that many of these 're-engineering' attempts fail, but while the disruption may not be justifiable in terms of productivity, such sharp, disruptive restructuring signals that change is for real, that the leadership is doing something about the difficulties which have become evident, and this is usually enough to bring about a rise in stock prices:

> While disruption may not be justifiable in terms of productivity, the short term returns to stockholders provide a strong incentive to the powers of chaos disguised by that seemingly reassuring word 'reengineering'. Perfectly viable businesses are gutted and abandoned, capable employees are set adrift rather than rewarded, simply because the organization must prove to the market that it is capable of change.
>
> (Sennett 1998: 51)

This may be a further reason for the importance of organization at a local level, where it is much easier for local field workers to maintain their focus on the children and parents they are paid to serve, untrammelled by the distractions of power relationships and political imperatives.

The organization, regulation and measurement of services: interruptions to intra- and interpersonal processes

For Sennett this trust relationship also has an intrapersonal component. To be trustworthy is to show some ongoing commitment, a commitment energized and sustained by underpinning principles. He notes that too often the modern workplace does not require 'principled action': it is set about with regulation. In the case of children's services, the social workers who joined the service in order to elaborate their own beliefs in justice and care spend much of their day explaining that the person referred, in obvious need of support, falls below their thresholds for intervention. Similarly, the teacher who intended to support young people in becoming confident and skilful adults, finds they have to 'deliver' a curriculum that is inappropriate for many of their children, and that the failure that results frequently converts into disaffection. In little time they move from facilitating self-actualization to mediating failure, and participating in social exclusion. Their own creative human response, drawing on the principles that inspired them to enter these professions, is not required of them.

The mechanisms for regulation and measurement

So what is it about the workplace that interrupts principle-led practice? O'Neil (2002: 45) in her Reith lecture series examined what has been called 'a crisis of trust'. She observes that

> the quest for accountability has penetrated all our lives, like great draughts of Heineken, reaching parts that supposedly less developed forms of accountability did not reach ... for those of us in the public service the new accountability takes the form of detailed control. An unending stream of new legislation and regulation ... they require detailed conformity to procedures and protocols, detailed record keeping and provision of information in specified formats and success in reaching targets ...

She points out that compliance reduces the amount of time that professionals can spend on their core role. Indeed, reducing the time spent on regulation picks up its own set of targets, for example targets to reduce the number of complaints procedures because the protocols that accompany them are so burdensome. She concludes that

> the new accountability is widely experienced not just as changing but (I think) as distorting the proper aims of professional practice and indeed as damaging professional pride and integrity. Much professional practice used to centre on interaction with those whom professionals serve: patients and pupils, students and families in need ...

> (O'Neil 2002: 50)

Similarly, Ball (2003) explores the role of what he calls 'performativity', a new mode of state regulation that requires individual practitioners to set aside personal values and commitments to organize themselves as a response to targets and indicators. He sees this mode of regulation as developing its own technologies and cultural norms, requiring compliance, because the judgements that follow from these processes have direct implications for future resourcing and

> as such they stand for, encapsulate and represent the worth, the quality or value of an individual or organization within a field of judgement ... The issue of who controls the field of judgement is crucial ... who is it that determines what is to count as valuable, effective or satisfactory performance and what measures or indicators are considered valid?
>
> (Ball 2003: 216)

In O'Neil's view, this new accountability is ostensibly for the benefit of the public but

> the real requirements are for accountability to regulators, to departments of governments, to funders, to legal standards. The new forms of accountability impose forms of central control – quite often indeed a range of different and mutually inconsistent forms of central control ... incompatible or barely compatible requirements invite compromises and evasions; they undermine professional judgement and institutional autonomy ...
>
> (O'Neil 2002: 53–4)

Ball, drawing on data from teachers talking about their experience of working within such cultures found that

> A kind of values schizophrenia is experienced by individual teachers where commitment, judgement and authenticity within practice are sacrificed for impression and performance. Here is a potential splitting between the teacher's own judgements about 'good practice' and students' 'needs' and the rigours of performance
>
> (Ball 2003: 221)

We heard similar concerns from practitioners distressed by what they felt to be the distortions of decision making required to meet the demands of an accountability culture. In contrast, we noted the role of the home school community link workers, so movingly appreciated by parents, who had a role too recently developed to have attracted regulation. They could focus on what was required of them, undistracted by procedures, protocols and targets, and respond as one human being to another.

This is not to say that accountability is unnecessary or that performance indicators are not an appropriate way of measuring performance, but rather to argue that they are 'performance indicators' not a complete account of the performance itself, still less a focus for intervention. Having established that teenage pregnancy rates, juvenile crime figures or GCSE results do give us interesting feedback on our policies for young people, it does not follow that we need to have specialist teams to work on teenage pregnancy, young people at risk of offending or children on the cusp of getting the right kind of GCSE result. The recent UNICEF (2007) report providing comparative data on children's well-being, found that of the 40 indicators used to compile the six key themes, teenage pregnancy was the single indicator that correlated most closely to the final accumulated outcome. Focusing on these young people may provide a rich source of data about what has gone wrong, but much earlier work is likely to be needed to reduce the number of people in the category.

Tipping the statistics may bring in extra resources, but at the same time it distorts the services that are being 'measured', resulting in the fragmentation of service provision. The targeting in itself is extremely problematic. For appropriate targeting to take place, assessment needs to be emphasized and tightly defined by the intervention to which it is linked. This leads to the idea that the expert professional can assess and remediate a particular need. All of this also leads to services being measured in terms of turnover and what they can fix, and for children and families to be defined as in need of fixing. Identifying those at 'risk' of teenage pregnancy or crime, cannot be achieved by any yet known screening test, we can only establish 'vulnerability' with multifactorial causes and multidimensional outcomes. As Freeman (1999) has argued, causative links become even more difficult to establish when we are implementing early interventions or preventative approaches. Furthermore, in identifying young people at any stage of their 'problem behaviour', we amplify their own, their families' and their communities' narrative of themselves as failing.

Risk and responsibility

The notion of 'risk' can provide a helpful tool for reviewing service provision and care pathways, but as a way of viewing individual lives it is problematic. 'Risk' is a relationship between a person or group of persons and their environment, and their environment is multidimensional. 'Risk' also builds and falls over time. If there is to be 'intervention' in a young person's life to build their 'resilience' or reduce their 'risk', it is crucially important to be able to view a range of these contexts and to track these over time.

Take the case of Paul, a rather middle of the road, unexceptional example of the support system in practice. Paul struggled with his learning and did not enjoy school; he was not especially difficult at school but after a year of secondary school, he preferred not to go. Instead, he hung out with older lads and joined in with their activities which included in his words 'robbing' and then often 'firing' cars. It became increasingly difficult for his mother to manage him and when he was 'got into' school his initial non-participation started to turn into behaviour that was difficult to manage. His relationship with his peers was poor because his social engagements were outside school. His absences had turned his original learning difficulties into a chronic gap in skills that made it difficult for him to access a secondary school curriculum. It became difficult to find positive aspects to his school life.

The school worked hard to make his experience there more relevant and to minimize his disruptive behaviour, but after two years of making such efforts, the school permanently excluded him. During the period building up to the exclusion, his offending activity resulted in his being considered for a support project focused on children under 14 who were in danger of entering the criminal justice system. Although on the edge of the age limit he received a place. This intervention involved a youth worker working with Paul and his mother and liaising with his schools during the period building up to a 'managed transfer'. It also included a mental health appraisal, but although there were some concerns, it was felt that the family context was too chaotic to successfully work with him. Support included working in a group with other similarly placed young people, and engaging in a variety of activities, for example go-karting, skating and paint-balling. This kind of activity provided an opportunity for the youth worker to support the young people in developing their social skills and reviewing the choices they were making in their lives. Paul particularly enjoyed these activities as it was the first time he had been able to do anything like this.

The intervention ended after five months. This was a longer period than the project usually supported, particularly as Paul was out of the age group soon after starting. In completing the 'piece of work' the youth worker made great efforts to ensure ongoing support from local youth centres. Six months after the intervention Paul and his mother talked very warmly about the relationship with the youth worker. His mother felt relationships had been much easier at home, but Paul had recently started going out with his old friends again and this was causing arguments between them, she wished he could see the youth worker again but appreciated he had had his turn and was now too old. Paul recognized the improved situation at home but also felt he was getting on better with others of his own age and spending less time with the lads with whom he was getting into trouble. Unfortunately, the 'managed school transfer' had broken down a few months after the support had stopped and Paul was, at the time of the review, being supported in a pupil referral unit. His key worker in the unit explained that he was fine in the small group setting of the unit but things broke down when he was placed in a school. The key worker had no idea that Paul had been involved in the project six months earlier. A subsequent review (three months later) has shown Paul was again in trouble with the police and his mother again felt out of her depth.

This story demonstrates patterns we frequently saw in our research. The youth worker support was only available following formal referral and panel procedures. Further, the referral process could not take place until certain criteria had been met, in this case the threat of exclusion and evidence of offending behaviour. Eighteen months prior to this intervention the school and the child's mother had identified that there was a real problem. However, at the point where the school was trying hard to galvanize support, Paul was not far enough up the tariff of need to receive the support that could have salvaged his school career. Without the additional support the school placement broke down. Following the withdrawal of the support that seemed to make a difference, Paul again found himself with a key worker, but one who didn't know the previous history and whom Paul didn't feel he trusted. Placed in a referral unit he drew down a lot more resources than would have been necessary if the youth worker had continued to work with him. If the youth worker had continued to work with him, the schools would almost certainly have managed to retain him and the more positive peer relationship he had started to develop could have been maintained. At the same time the mental health issues that were identified were never dealt with because the only mental health provision available required a more 'stable family context' than Paul had. The system Paul came across was primarily focused on the 'fair' allocation of resources and the delivery of preformed services rather than the meeting of his needs. As a result it was very expensive to provide him with a poor deal from the system. He received an intervention that made a difference and showed his capability for change, but it was not sustained for long enough to create a real turning point for him.

The services that target these 'at risk' young people usually identify them at the point at which 'risk' turns into inevitability which is arguably too late for effective intervention to take place. Services are fragmented and so not only is communication made more difficult between each fragment but young people fall through the gaps in provision. The lack of continuity of provision frequently results in 'a good piece of work' unravelling because the small amounts of support necessary for consolidating change are not available. The young person's situation has to deteriorate enough to result in further provision kicking in. Nobody oversees the period between the 'good pieces of work' and the more upstream support systems that could provide the continuity. Community youth provision, for example, is not universally available or is struggling on short-term, 'shoestring' resources. It could be argued that, as a community, we are failing to provide effective support for troubled children and young people until they express their distress in obviously antisocial ways.

If the fragmentation of services creates problems for communication between field workers, it creates even more problems for the way children going through the system are perceived. Viewing the young person as 'a case' that can be opened and closed, interrupts feelings of long-term responsibility for young people and distracts from a proper analysis of their own particular ongoing needs.

Linking individual relationships and community responsibility: providing a context in which mutual trust and commitment can develop

We have already discussed how local systems are necessary to improve communication, but it is also crucially important for individual field workers to feel the responsibility for the ongoing support for the child, to not drop the baton until it is securely taken on by someone else. Indeed, to feel that there will be someone else to pass the baton on to. We would argue that this can only happen successfully when there is a climate of trust, when there is a communal responsibility for the lives of children and young people on a particular patch. Further, that this communal responsibility cannot be left to chance but needs to be mapped into the communication system at the level of the local patch.

Fulfilling this communal responsibility is assisted when there is a relevant community for children to be welcomed back into. Moss and Petrie (2002) argue that much of what we attempt to contribute to children's lives through 'children's services' could be better achieved through rethinking 'children's spaces'. They argue for a greater consideration to be given to the kinds of community spaces that children inhabit and how we can enhance them. In Chapter 4, we reviewed the way the link workers effectively connect children and their carers into such community resources. However, it was disturbing to see how limited and fragile these were. Almost all 'the resources' were short-term projects funded by the Children's Fund or projects that had received start-up money from the Children's Fund that were now holding together on a thread with committed field workers spending hours of their own time bidding to achieve shoestring funding.

It is also interesting to note here, that there is a real divide in the quantity and richness of experiences outside of school across socio-economic boundaries. While some children have their time, arguably, over-organized by enthusiastic parents, others have nothing to do and no money to buy into the limited subsidized resources that are available. It seems unfortunate that we only provide youth support and positive and exciting activities for young people after they have fired a few cars.

While Moss and Petrie are particularly concerned with the way we envision and expand children's spaces outside the time regulated by the school, they are also concerned about the time spent in the dominant space of childhood, that of the school. They draw on Dewey's (1897: 80) critique of the school environment, more than a century ago:

> I believe that much of present education fails because it neglects this fundamental principle of the school as a form of community life. It conceives the school as a place where certain information is to be given, where certain lessons are to be learned, or where certain habits are to be formed. The value of these is conceived as lying largely in the remote future; the child must do these things for the sake of something else he is to do; they are mere preparation. As a result they do not become a part of the life experience of the child and so are not truly educative.

Prout (2000: 305) pursues this tension in the current discourse of childhood in relation to 'the way that modernity has emphasized childhood as a period of the life course oriented towards the future'. In this connection Prout considers the government's concern with child poverty. Here, while welcoming the concern and intention to abolish child poverty, he questions the underlying rationale for the policy, noting that it draws heavily on longitudinal studies linking childhood circumstances to adult outcomes:

> It is shown that poverty and disadvantage in childhood are precursors to educational and labour market failures in later life.

The central focus is on the better adult lives that will, it is predicted, emerge from reducing child poverty. It is not on the better lives that children will lead as children.

(Prout 2000: 305)

For the many children like Paul, who are failing to learn in our schools, we provide little for the *living present* or the *remote future*, and it is not hard to see how he might choose not to participate or why 'firing' cars might be an exciting highlight to an otherwise rather bleak existence. By focusing on the individual child, we are distracted from examining the contexts that may be generating some of the needs they are themselves required to fix. Children themselves, when consulted, tend to press for changes in the quality of universal provision. When asked, for example, about 'the school I'd like' (Birkett, cited in Burke and Grosvenor 2005), their proposals were such that would make their childhoods in the here and now more inclusive, safer and more aesthetically pleasing. Evaluations from the local Children's Fund presented a clear view that it was the extension of universal services that they felt would have made a difference: 'schools where teachers smile more', 'places to go that didn't cost anything'. As Moss and Petrie (2002) argue 'spaces' not 'services'.

Field workers are absolutely central to quality provision and successful outcomes for children, young people and their families. The different values, training and life experiences they bring to their work can result in an enriching of their contribution to working with individuals, groups and the contexts in which they are situated. Equally, this same complexity can be a cause of conflict, misunderstanding and a failure of trust. The difference seems to rest on their opportunities for dialogue and their scope for action. Where they have sufficient opportunities to make sense of their own experience with other field workers, and sufficient scope to respond creatively together in ways that draw on, or at least do not conflict with, their own core values, they feel positively about their experiences together and the system in which they are operating. Our studies did not have the scope to link these findings to better outcomes for children and, indeed, Percy-Smith (2006) reviewing the research on partnership, had difficulty finding evidence of the impact of partnership working for children and young people. However, some American research does suggest that positive working contexts do directly link to better outcomes for the people they are designed to serve.

Hemmelgarn et al. (2006: 75), in a review of studies on organiza-tional culture and climate in 'human service systems' in America, define organizational culture as 'the shared norms, beliefs and behavioural expectations that drive behaviour and communicate what is valued in organizations'.

Their conclusions from an extensive review of the literature indicate that

> Culture and climate mould the nature, tone, and focus of the relationships and interactions between service provider and service recipient ... If a work environment is non-supportive, impersonal and stressful, employees' interactions with those who receive their services will reflect the lack of support, impersonality, and stress ...
>
> (Hemmelgarn et al. 2006: 75–8)

On the other hand, the evidence Hemmelgarn et al. draw upon shows that

> Children who are served by agencies with more positive climates are more likely to experience improved pychosocial functioning, obtain more comprehensive services, and experience more continuity in the services they receive ... Caseworkers in more positive climates provide services with higher levels of responsiveness and availability to the children they serve.
>
> (2006: 79)

There is a much larger literature on the links between working climate and outcomes in business studies as, for example, in Owen's (1996) intriguing study of the dynamics of the Red Arrows team. In this study, the team was tightly knit and the required outcomes are very clearly defined and so in many ways unlike the loose-knit and complex contexts that workers in children's services operate within. However, the issue of trust and the importance of high quality outcomes were similarly key. At the same time there was similarity in that the joint performance depended on the coordination of individual effort and different specialist roles in potentially high-risk situations. Owen identifies a number of key conditions underpinning the excellence of the team:

- involvement in decision making;
- openness in communication;
- the importance of feedback;
- opportunities for dialogue;
- pride in and commitment to joint working;
- developing individual potential.

Owen observed the way in which each member of the team was involved in setting goals, defining strategies and selecting new members, and the importance of this in ensuring feelings of ownership and commitment to the project. It was important that each team member could realize their own personal goals in the team's goals. Similarly, in the effective forums we saw examples of ownership and the commitment that resulted, and although there were no specific selection procedures, the good 'system minders' we identified had often emerged as respected practitioners rather than being subject to any formal selection procedures. This was in contrast to the 'collaborative inertia' that we observed where the system wasn't working and nobody seemed to have the power to do anything about it, exemplified by the frustration that established groups experienced when coordinators were shipped in from outside the area without any local consultation.

Owen noted the importance of the generation of pride and commitment for effective joint working but also the importance of individuals taking responsibility for the successful completion of their role in relation to the whole project. For pride and commitment to develop, the project has to have a shape, and for many in children's services that shape is their individual 'piece of work'. Where the local 'patch' was working well, this provided an identifiable unit with which to identify jointly.

Further, one of the features of the local forums was the opportunities for dialogue and the possibilities for providing feedback about how these individual 'pieces of work' contributed to the group effort. We saw many examples of this in our data. For example, two educational psychologists had been concerned about working to the agenda of the school consultation team (SCT), but on reflection on their experience of working in different SCTs, both found that they received positive feedback from the team about the value of their particular contribution to discussion. They had previously been seen as gatekeepers to resources, but in the SCT discussions, other group members came to value the particular contributions that they could make as psychologists. They feared losing their professional identity, but actually found it enhanced, and explicitly valued in a way they had not previously experienced. This fear of professional identity being undermined is also mentioned by Anning et al. (2006) as a factor to be considered in developing multiprofessional teams.

The local forums also provided a context for another factor that Owen saw as important: the ongoing development of each team member's potential so that 'when a person knows they are growing and doing well and it is recognized ... the team members set a standard of performance and each strives towards that' (Owen 1996: 114).

Perceived 'gaps in provision' could often be met by field workers volunteering to reconfigure their roles and receiving staff development opportunities to do so. The orchestration of the 'system minder' provides an overview that allows team members to be supported in developing their own potential within the context of enhancing the contributions of the individual to the work of the 'patch' as a whole. If people are to be tempted out of their silos, they have to feel the new space they are being encouraged to enter is a relatively safe and interesting place to be.

7 Conclusions: the dynamics of complexity

In their book *The Structure of Magic*, Bandler and Grinder (1975) describe how they set about defining the qualities of a good psychotherapist. They had noted that there were a number of very highly regarded therapists who seemed to be able to bring about transforming change in those who came to them. However, curiously, they did not seem to share a theoretical approach or a common training regime. What they shared was a reputation for being effective and being held in high esteem by clients and colleagues. Bandler and Grinder wanted to see whether, despite the apparent differences of approach, there were some underlying similarities of practice. They wanted to find the structure of the magic that these particular therapists seemed to be able to perform.

Similarly, we had seen multiprofessional practice that seemed to work, where field workers engaged successfully in encouraging positive change in the children and families with whom they were working, while at the same time feeling supported and safe themselves. We had also seen very similar multiprofessional contexts that achieved the opposite. We set out to observe a range of different contexts in which the apparently successful and less successful practice was embedded. Drawing on data from six different local areas and three specialist provisions, we found varying degrees of effectiveness in the systems for communication and interaction. In order to establish 'success' we looked at these local systems in terms of Huxham and Vangen's (2005) analytical framework of *collaborative advantage* and *collaborative inertia*.

Our dataset is small but the patterns we have found consistently recur. Further, they seem to replicate the findings of other researchers, looking at similarly complex organizational structures, in a range of settings (Vickers [1965] 1995; Huxham and Vangen 2005; Hemmelgarn et al. 2006). Rather more controversially, they demonstrate the patterns of complexity found across a wide range of biological and social organizational systems, the study of which has been influential in our analysis.

Recognizing the dynamics of complexity

When groups of people are engaged in related activities, a pattern of interaction and communication inevitably develops or *emerges*. Over time the relationships become systematically organized. This organization will be influenced by what are known as the *attractors* in the system of relationships, that is, features of the system that focus or draw in the interaction. Examples of such *attractors* are often linked to the allocation of resources, for example statementing procedures and target setting. These features are intended to direct behaviour, but in so doing they create unexpected side effects. The system left to self-organize will shape, or distort, itself in relation to these features. Further, individual interactions will be subject to *amplification* and *attenuation* of effect depending on individual characteristics, such as power status, or interactional characteristics, such as levels of trust. Thus, the outcomes of such an organization are non-linear and impossible to predict. Left to self-organize, the dynamics of the system may result in an organizational culture that does not facilitate the intended aims of its participants. When this happens the participants' experience leads them to feel 'the system isn't working'. Conversely the dynamics of the system can produce more positive and creative outcomes than could have been anticipated.

Developing appreciative systems

The distinctive feature of the systems where we found the multi-professional practice seemed to be working successfully, was that the field workers were in a position to reflect on the organizational contexts in which they were operating. Through this reflection, they were able collaboratively to continually make small changes to the configurations of the system to ensure their central purposes were being negotiated and maintained. In doing so they created what Vickers ([1965] 1995) has called, an 'appreciative system'.

To enhance this reflective capacity, they set up opportunities for communication and allocated specific responsibilities to 'mind the system'. Thus, in the examples we saw, link workers and youth workers were minding the system of relationships around a child, involving peers, family, field workers and the school. Similarly the school consultation team (SCT) was minding the system around the school, so that the school staff and the range of field workers were able to improve their joint capacity to meet the needs of the children in their care. At the level of the local 'patch' the information from the field workers and the school consultation teams was brought together to review the workings of the local system as a whole. These local data were further enriched, in some areas, by the addition of parents' groups or children's groups feeding directly into the forum discussions. The issues and understandings developed at these local forums could in turn be represented and discussed in wider local authority groupings.

Thus well configured communication systems, 'appreciative systems', seemed to be crucial to successful multiprofessional practice. Our findings also suggest a relationship between the success of these systems and the extent to which they were locally initiated and sustained. Local ownership seemed to be a necessary prerequisite to their development. We speculate that being an active member of an appreciative system, in a position to share in the reflection upon and to address the problems of a particular 'patch', allowed individuals to feel they could contribute to the group endeavour and to feel they were accountable for it.

The local forums provided an environment that supported reflective, collaborative practice allowed differences in values to surface and, if effectively 'minded', to be aired and resolved over time. Importantly, it seemed that if the opportunities for good quality dialogue are available, the differences are not perceived to be a barrier, but rather as stimulating and a challenge to the development of thinking about future policy and practice. At the same time, where the local 'patch' was working well, it provided a definable unit with which field workers could jointly identify. For individuals to feel pride and commitment in their work that work needs to be identifiable and to have a shape. We had often seen this expressed in the notion of 'a good piece of work' (discussed in Chapter 6). Where this joint identity began to emerge and become established, field workers began to talk in terms of joint activity and joint responsibility and in so doing were able to accept the need for 'norm holding' and the 'taking up' of personal responsibility within the group as a whole. Given that the effectiveness of work with children, young people and their families depends to a great extent on the quality of the relationships they experience from field workers, maintaining the morale and commitment of these field workers is of central importance.

The 'appreciative system' also provided continuity in the viewing of children and families and opportunities for the systemic and sustained support that an accumulation of risk factors requires. It ensured that 'a good piece of work' did not unravel because the small amounts of support necessary for consolidating change were not available. The early concerns raised by those working in schools could be seen and heard by those with specialist skills who would previously have not come across the children until much later in their care pathway. This provided schools with an external gaze and support in the consideration of alternative approaches to the ways they work with children on the margins. It also provided possibilities for continuity of support from the point where the school placement starts to fail. It provided a context where the boundaries between services can be negotiated and where the baton of responsibility can be safely transferred from one field worker to another.

Nested systems: keeping the communication flowing

The communication systems we found were nested in a way that allowed the crucial insights from the ground, through a series of feedback loops, to feed into local authority decision making. However, this last step in the communication system was fragile. One of the things we observed was the way in which these good local systems were continually limited by the difficulties of getting resolution at the next level. While some messages influenced decision making, there were no formal channels for the communication to take place and so there was only a partial uptake of issues and concerns. While there was potential for this rich local data to become the basis for local authority decision making, in reality the uptake of ideas tended only to take place when they fitted in with current local authority thinking. Confirmatory evidence was amplified, but evidence that challenged developing policy was attenuated.

Indeed, we found a number of other features of these systems that were problematic for local authority policy makers. First, they seemed to be difficult to create to order, through restructuring from above. They seemed, in short, to need to evolve rather than to be designed. As they evolved they were able to draw on local strengths of personnel and provision. They were able to shape themselves according to their own particular geography and economy. Perhaps most important, the process of evolving practice together generated feelings of empowerment, ownership and responsibility.

Second, the four most successful examples we studied were very differently configured. Although they shared the underlying principles of the communication structures described in the example above, they looked rather different from each other. However, beneath the differences they all functioned to provide a local forum for discussion of issues around the needs of children, young people and their families in identifiable communities. Where community needs were higher, and more people needed to collaborate, the communication structures were more differentiated and more tightly structured. Where needs were lower the communication structures were more loose knit.

Third, the rushed timescale required for compliance to central government policy drivers, and the complexity of the multiprofessional agenda, has made it difficult for managers to resist adopting more than usually top-down management at local authority level. While the government has recognized, in implementing the ECM agenda, the difficulties of controlling the complexity of multiprofessional services and the need for this to be managed locally, local authorities themselves have had little time to consider what 'locality' means and how they might adapt their leadership practices to meet the demands of managing such locally driven systems.

Managing locally driven systems

If these evolving, appreciative, locally driven systems are desirable, what is the role of local authority management in enabling them to flourish? Our analysis suggests the following key roles:

- to lead the dialogue about values;
- to receive and process feedback and evaluate and frame policy;
- to engender ownership in localities;
- to ensure quality and accountability.

Leading the dialogue about values

One of the problems that seems to make multiprofessional work stressful for practitioners is what Ball (2003) has called *a kind of values schizophrenia* (see Chapter 6, p. 99), which causes field workers to feel that what they are required to do conflicts with their own value system. At the same time, field workers are working together with others holding different values, and they do not have the time to explore or understand these differences. One of the features of the more successful communication systems, was that field workers were able to make explicit some of these underpinning values and begin to share a vision of what this dialogue might mean in terms of providing a better future for children and families on their 'patch'. The *Every Child Matters* 'five outcomes for children' provides a broad and helpful framework for this discussion, but it is not always clear how these outcomes are understood and translated through local policy and practice. The relationship between policy and practice, and the underpinning principles that inform both, are important to discuss at all levels of the organization.

Schumacher (1974: 54), in his classic polemic on the optimum size of organizations, makes a clear case for distinguishing between the proper sites for agreeing action and those for for agreeing principles:

> We always need both freedom and order. We need the freedom of lots and lots of small autonomous units, and, at the same time, the orderliness of large scale, possibly global, unity and co-ordination. When it comes to action we obviously need small units because action is a highly personal affair and one cannot be in touch with more than a very limited number of persons at one time. But when it comes to the world of ideas, to principles or to ethics . . . we need to recognize the unity of mankind and base our actions on this recognition . . . what I wish to emphasize is the duality of the human requirement when it comes to size . . . for his different purposes man needs many different structures . . . for every activity there is a certain appropriate scale . . .

Making explicit the principles which guide actions is at the root of achieving mutual understanding. So it is an important function of local authority leadership to set up the contexts in which those principles and underpinning values can be debated and negotiated.

Receiving and processing feedback, and evaluating and framing policy

Schumacher contrasts the importance of leading on the debate about values and principles with providing freedom at the level of field workers' actions, and this resonates with our findings on the importance of 'patch' working. Receiving a continual flow of feedback from local areas, acted upon at local authority level, should avoid the longstanding frustrations that were evident in the systems that were not working. This in turn allows the most problematic constraints in the system to be addressed, so that everyone has a positive experience of moving forward even as new challenges inevitably present themselves. Most significantly, the continual flow of evidence will facilitate changes in the framework of service delivery to ensure children receive support that is timely and appropriate. At the same time the institutions that provide environments for children will be developed to better meet their needs.

This flow of evidence highlights the earlier discussion about values, because in order to provide a positive environment for children we have first to establish what a good childhood should be, and what needs to change to get closer to making this possible. We have to decide on the extent to which the universal provision is inclusive and configured as a suitable habitat for what Dewey has referred to as the 'living present' of all children.

The local authority will be mediating a range of perspectives and practices coming from localities and balancing these with the management of central government imperatives. At the same time the local authority is well positioned, with good quality feedback systems, to be the conduit for ideas from the localities to reach and influence central government policies – thereby completing the feedback loop. Indeed, recent policy relating to children would suggest that greater assertion from the ground would be, at least in principle, more likely to be welcomed now than in the past.

Hodgkin and Newell (1996), in their seminal report *Effective Government: Structures for Children*, proposed ways of ensuring that central government is responsive to children's needs. Many of their proposals have been taken forward: the restructuring of government departments to focus policy making for children in one place; the appointment of children's commissioners; a children's minister (2003) and, as of June 2007, a secretary of State for Children, Schools and Families (DCSF). However, as Payne (2007) reports, while there have been these important structural changes, less progress has been made in terms of functions. She points out that Hodgkin and Newell also 'explored the concept of child impact assessment in which proposals for policy, legislation, service restructuring, planning or monitoring are analysed for their potential impact on children and young people' (1996: 471).

Child impact assessment, now promoted by the UN Committee on the Rights of the Child (CRC), is a means whereby signatory nations review and assess proposals for policy and legislation for their potential impact on children and young people. In view of the amount of legislation which affects children, child impact assessment has the potential to increase very significantly awareness of children's rights in Parliament and elsewhere. 'Perhaps more importantly,' Payne adds, 'child impact assessment has identified issues which inhibit shared policy development across government departments' (2007: 475). Linking child impact assessment, she suggests, as in Sweden, with the implementation of the CRC, notably article 3 (best interests of the child), article 2 (non-discrimination), article 6 (child survival and development) and article 12 (child's right to express his or her views), would seem to suggest a principled way forward for the development of policies through which to achieve the outcomes hoped for from *Every Child Matters*. It would also be as appropriate an exercise at local authority level as it is at national level.

Engendering ownership in localities

If, as our studies suggest, communication systems were successful to the extent that they are locally organized, a major challenge for local authorities would be to engender a climate in which local ownership could develop. Paradoxically, local forums are simple and inexpensive to set up, but they do require ample time for agreement to be reached on what is understood locally by 'a locality'. And this understanding needs to be one that is shared among all parties: field workers, children and families, and local authorities. Once localities are geographically explicit, all they require is encouragement for people in a local area to look very carefully at what is currently happening, to look at how this is perceived by the communities that are being served and to look at small changes that might shift the whole system into producing something better. Perhaps even more significantly in so doing, the knowledge already gained by the system, the relationships already long established, will not be lost by disruptive re-organization.

The local authority can encourage this process by amplifying emergent efforts to develop the communication system and attenuating policy and practice that gets in the way of forum development: precisely the kind of sensitive system minding role that we have described earlier for the successful running of localities. The local authority can further assist by building on current communication structures and encouraging the emergence of local leadership, people with the kind of 'relational power' that will enable them to take on a local system minding role.

We saw examples of clusters of schools taking just such initiatives. In one case for example, a head teacher, having experienced the value of a local network in his previous school, set up a network for a cluster of schools in his new area. He simply arranged a meeting for local field workers for an hour at lunchtime, organized a focus for discussion for the meeting and worked with colleagues to prepare field workers in advance about the purposes of a network. Two years later the network continues to have regular, well attended, meetings drawing on a wide range of field workers across schools, children's services, health and voluntary organizations.

Working towards subsidiarity

In our studies the biggest constraint on the development of effective communication systems was the inflexibility of funding streams. This meant that there was very little opportunity for localities to develop their provision to meet the issues and concerns that were being discussed in their forums, beyond that which they could raise themselves by pooling the resources from individual schools. This is an area where the local authority could make a crucial difference through leading on discussions of subsidiarity, that is, the delegation of funding to the most meaningful local organizational structure. They could, for example, provide opportunities for localities to bid for joint funding and, when they are operating healthily, devolve extended services funding to the locality.

Schools have been operating in local 'clusters' and 'partnerships' for many years in some authorities (Lunt et al. 1994; McConnell 1994). However, this has less often resulted in devolved funding at the level of the cluster, with the tendency being either to hold resources at the centre or for them to go direct to individual schools. Nevertheless, some authorities have been conducting bolder experiments for some time, including substantial delegation to the cluster – for example in Nottinghamshire (Cade and Caffyn 1994, 1995) and Norfolk (Beek 2002).

Given the documented success of such projects, it is surprising that these practices have not become more widespread. However, this is perhaps an inevitable consequence of cross-currents in government policy. Even as these school partnerships were emerging, Gray and Dessent (1993) were drawing attention to the increasing culture of competition that was threatening their development. With the standards debate there has been further encouragement for schools to see each other within a competitive framework, often gaining an advantage in the league tables by shedding their more vulnerable and troublesome members. As resources are devolved to schools, and local authorities shrink, the local authority agenda becomes less relevant to schools. At the same time the increasing differentiation and complexity of individual school structures makes clustering less likely and as a result many schools are moving away from a sense of themselves as part of a resource to the community in which the community has a stake. The excellence of the *Every Child Matters* framework may yet be fatally damaged by the move away from the notion of the community school. Notwithstanding this increasingly depressing backdrop to the ECM policy, local forums remain the best hope for effective communication systems and school clusters the best opportunity for ensuring it can be resourced.

Resisting the temptation to impose a one-size-fits-all model

A further challenge for local authorities in supporting the development of localities is the lack of, and indeed the irrelevance of, a 'one size fits all' model. The dynamics of complexity mean that a particular configuration with identical properties can never occur in the same way twice. At the same time the very nature of local ownership means the evolving communication systems will develop out of local strengths. In our examples this was sometimes led by the secondary school, but as often the galvanizing energy came from groups of primary schools or the local children's centre. As the communication systems developed different elements of the cluster and different personnel within the cluster led the process, so that the localities showed themselves to be surprisingly resilient in the face of particular institutions waxing and waning and particular individuals moving on.

Examples of successful leadership arrangements for the forums included: a head teacher working closely with a link worker; a school counsellor supported by an education social worker and a health visitor; a secondary SEN coordinator supported by a small multiprofessional steering group; an EAZ manager supported by a local special school head teacher; a children's centre head working in conjunction with two primary heads; two primary school heads sharing the role; and a primary head in tandem with a local authority adviser.

For local authorities this variation can seem problematic, raising concerns about whether everyone is getting an equal deal, and raising the question of what needs to be held tight and what can be left loose to be resolved at a local level. From the evidence we collected, the local forum, however configured, would seem to meet the requirements of the consistent organizational hub. The forum can demonstrate how all the members of the community can be represented and have clear duties in relation to, for example, local decision making, evaluation and quality assurance issues. But the levels of complexity involved prevent the presentation of any complete models of good practice. As Dewey ([1900/43] 1990: 94) argues, 'A working model is not something to be copied; it is to afford a demonstration of the feasibility of the principle and of the methods that make it feasible'.

Ensuring quality and accountability

To meet the essentially collaborative approach that *Every Child Matters* engenders, all local authority services for children and young people will be subject to a 'joint area review', directed by the Office for Standards in Education (DfES 2005). This review of joint provision will require judgements on:

- how well local children's centres, schools and services are promoting the five outcomes for children and young people;
- the effectiveness of the protection of vulnerable children;
- the extent to which service providers are able to reflect upon their own practices and identify their own strengths and weaknesses;
- the extent to which the views of children and parents are being heard in decision making about services.

We have already argued that local forums are well placed to produce the kind of feedback to support such an inspection process. Generating good quality data at local level avoids the dangers of generic evaluation, which tends to neutralize findings of good and weak practice by averaging the results of everything thrown into the data pot. Local evaluation processes can be directly drawn upon for the local authority's annual performance assessment (APA) that feeds into the joint review process. And local forums can make contributions and responses to the drafting of their local authority's Children and Young People's plan.

Local forums have the potential for engaging the perspectives of children and their families in a genuine commentary on local provision, which in turn can be fed back into decision making at a local level. Indeed, such local participation would seem to be the best hope of meeting the legal requirement stated in the Children Acts (1989, 2004) to consult children in decisions which affect their lives. Local forums also offer the possibility of listening carefully to the people who are engaging most closely with children and their families: the youth workers and link workers who often provide the most sustained and satisfying support.

Local organization enables the possibility of evaluating communication systems, particular provision and individual outcomes for children all within the same framework using the 'upstream–downstream' analysis. Thus individual care pathways can be considered against a particular context. This avoids the tendency to locate the problem with the child, or the group of children with a particular named 'condition', and to organize fragmented provision around the children with the most noticeable or identifiable problems. It enables a consideration of the whole system and a critical evaluation of contexts as well as children. In so doing it also allows the consideration of the fitness of community resources for all children.

We noted in our evaluations some problems generated by an overreliance on targets as shapers of services as opposed to general indicators of successful outcomes for children (see the discussion in Chapter 6) and the local authority would seem to be best placed as a crucial mediator of the effective use of target setting. Goldratt (2006) points out the dynamics of the distortions created by target setting in his quip 'tell me how you will measure me and I will tell you how I will behave'. Flecknoe (2001: 218) expresses similar concerns but in his case for that which is left out of the analysis, 'what happens to the important but unmeasurable outcomes of education when the measurable outcomes have been improved'.

These systemic problems are explored by Power (1997: 123), who concludes: 'The audit society is a society that endangers itself because it invests too heavily in shallow rituals of verification at the expense of other forms of organizational intelligence . . .'.

Such other forms of organizational intelligence in relation to children's services, would seem to us to be precisely the reflective discussions of field workers in local forums, well positioned to unpick the complexity of the experiences of the children and families whom they serve. Chaffin (2006), in a commentary on a series of papers looking at the challenges to evidence-based practice in America, notes that organizations that are orientated towards looking for results or measurable outcomes, and are committed to continual improvement, will be likely to assure quality provision: 'We might even speculate that an organizational culture committed to rigorous outcome testing will evolve in the direction of effective services regardless of which treatments it initially deploys' (Chaffin 2006: 92).

Power argues for the importance of taking personal responsibility as the core of effective quality assurance, and of the creation of environments where these habits of mind can be nurtured: 'It would be wrong to conclude simply that less auditing is desirable. The issue is rather a question of organizational design capable of bringing in "moral competence" and of providing regulated forms of openness around these competencies' (Power 1997: 144). The pressures on all services to reach targets and protect themselves from the results of falling short, tends to create exactly the self-protective culture that militates against such 'moral' competence.

Researching multiprofessional practice

We have argued in this book for more attention to be given to the whole system of relationships in which individual case work with children is embedded. This is in contrast to much current research into the effectiveness of children's services which has focused on an aspect of the system, such as the intervention, the service or the multiprofessional team. Todd (2007: 89) questions the emphasis on what she refers to as this 'service delivery' model: 'such a model implies that the child or family need fixing . . . this is a deficit rather than a strengths approach . . . [which sees] all the problems as inherent in the individual rather than a complex interaction of social practices and institutional, political and cultural influences.'

As well as Todd's concerns about the decontextualized nature of some research, there is also confusion about terminology. Frost (2005) provides a very helpful examination of a range of terminology associated with joint working and comments: 'one of the problems in writing and speaking about joined up thinking is that our language for conceptualising it is complex, confusing and imprecise' (p. 21). This conceptual confusion is particularly important because of the way terminology can frame thinking. While we were conducting our research we were aware of the frequent use of terms referring to teams and teamwork, for example 'multiprofessional teams', 'the team around the child' (Siraj-Blatchford et al. 2007), 'the locality team', but we were puzzled about how the word 'team' related to what we actually saw in practice. 'Teamwork' was clearly visible around particular designated conditions, as reported by, for example, Atkinson et al. (2001) but only a small minority of children involved with children's services come into this category, usually those with the greatest levels of complexity. Specialist expertise was often developed in teams, among, for example, the people with specialist skills that work across the local authority: the 'looked after team', the 'behaviour support team' and so on. But while these people trained together, they were rarely doing teamwork or case work together.

In the local communication systems we observed, even those elements referred to as teams, for example the 'school consultation teams', were only meeting together five or six times a year. The communication hubs in general were characterized by inclusive membership and regular but infrequent meetings, therefore too loose knit to deserve the designation 'team'. For comparison, Muir (1984: 170) defines a team as 'the continuous interaction between a small clearly bounded group of the same people who share a common task, similar values and who hold distinctive knowledge and skills'.

At the same time, teams are expensive and not easily connected to individual children and families – who need the time, continuity and relationship better achieved by responsive individual field work. We were reminded of Huxham and Vangen's (2005: 80) advice that 'unless potential for real collaborative advantage is clear, it is generally best, if there is a choice, to avoid collaboration'. And indeed our own findings that 'collaboration was less about collaborative activity, than about communicating effectively about individual pieces of work, ensuring the patchwork of individual effort in relation to a particular family, makes sense'.

There were many meetings attempting to communicate about individual pieces of work, to support the process of case work, and we were left with the feeling that it is these meetings and the way they link to the communication system as a whole, rather than the analysis of team functioning, that needs to be the focus of further research. Some of the meetings of this type seemed to be very effective and others less so. The size, regularity and purpose of meetings would seem to be an important factor in the achievement of 'collaborative advantage' as opposed to 'collaborative inertia'. Indeed the whole question of how case work is conducted, who conducts it and how the Common Assessment Framework and the notion of the lead professional impacts on this case work are pressing questions to resolve.

However, these cannot be considered outside the communication systems to which they contribute, so that case work doesn't reify the case as being 'the problem' and thus the only subject of scrutiny, rather it is the context from which the case is drawn. Data on the relationship between risk and disadvantage show that children are ten times more likely to have been in trouble with the police in the last year if they have five or more family disadvantages as opposed to those with no family disadvantages (Hoxhallari et al. 2007). Interestingly, this rate of offending behaviour is also twice as likely as for children with four family disadvantages. However, these offending children are only 10 per cent of the children who have five or more family disadvantages. The implication is that we need to look as much at the 90 per cent who do not offend as at the 10 per cent who do, in order to find out what really makes a difference to building resilience or falling into the offending category. This evidence supports the contention made earlier that upstream–downstream are part of the same river.

Similarly, the effectiveness of the case work cannot be judged without feedback about the experiences of those it is set up to help: more generally, we need to respond to the concerns of children themselves. For example, data from Oxfordshire Children and Young People's Survey 2007, including the views of 6539 children and young people (CYPB 2007), raises a number of issues with respect to the context of the lives of children and young people. While reporting back very positively on some aspects of their lives, for example their contributions to local conservation projects, the data showed that: 31 per cent of students in years 7 to 11 felt their local park was not safe; 44 per cent of primary children have been bullied, threatened, kicked or punched in the last year (and this rises to 51 per cent in secondary school); 35 per cent of children in years 7 to 11 don't think they have a say in the way things are run in school, as opposed to 31 per cent who do.

Among children in years 7 to 11 who live in temporary accommodation (figures in brackets show the comparison with the sample as a whole):

- 33% have bunked off school (17%);
- 66% had nothing or crisps/chocolate/fizzy drinks for breakfast on the day of the survey (20%);
- 32% have been bullied out of school (9%);

- 64% have special help for learning or behavioural needs (12%);
- 53% never sit down for a family meal (7%);
- 26% plan to leave school as soon as possible (7%).

These kinds of data show the problems of atomizing our support for these young people, focusing our attention only on their educational and extreme safety needs, or viewing them as 'cases' that can be opened and closed, depending on thresholds and protocols. A holistic view is essential, with the freedom to respond as fellow human beings both to the individual and to their environment, providing the opportunities for the 'capabilities' of ordinary children and their families to be realized. As Capra (1996: 29.30) has argued:

The great shock of twentieth-century science has been that systems cannot be understood by analysis. The properties of the parts are not intrinsic properties, but can be understood only within the context of the larger whole. Thus the relationship between the parts and the whole are reversed. In the systems approach, the properties of the parts can be understood only from the organization of the whole. Accordingly, systems thinking does not concentrate on the basic building-blocks but rather on the basic principles of organization. Systems thinking is 'contextual', which is the opposite of analytical thinking. Analysis means taking something apart in order to understand it; systems thinking means putting it into the context of a larger whole.

Everything we have observed about the relationships between field workers and field workers, and field workers and the children and families with whom they work, suggests the strength and possibilities of individual commitment and systems thinking, of seeing the parts within a larger whole. Perhaps we can best conclude by drawing on the passionate witness of Batmanghelidjh (2006: 157) – working at the furthest downstream extremities, with children who have fallen through the net of provision because of, she believes, a collective lack of will on the part of society:

As a society we have become diffident of being individually effective. We hide behind the comforting belief that the task is beyond us, that one individual cannot make a significant difference ... We are afraid when others show care, when they stand up for something valuable. We mistake homogeny for efficiency and force our services to lose the brilliant contribution of those who are kind ... we minimize the truth and as a group we deaden the space where creative solutions could thrive.

The children's data we discussed above are not just a matter for concern, but require urgent engagement. The individual 'good pieces of work' need to be connected up, and this is possible, not by yet another re-organization, but by the taking of personal responsibility and the gentle tweaking of the systems of which we are all a part. We have seen people making the system work for children.

References

Alldred, P., David, M. and Edwards, R. (2002) Minding the gap: children and young people negotiating relations between home and school, in R. Edwards (ed.) *Children, Home and School: Regulation, Autonomy or Connection?* London: RoutledgeFalmer.

Anning, A., Cottrell, D., Frost, N., Green, J. M. and Robinson, M. (2006) *Developing Multiprofessional Teamwork for Integrated Children's Services.* Maidenhead: Open University Press/McGraw-Hill Education.

Atkinson, M., Wilkin, A., Stott, A. and Kinder, K. (2001) *Multi-agency Working: An Audit Activity.* Slough: NFER.

Audit Commission (2002) *Statutory Assessment and Statements of SEN: In Need of Review?* London: Audit Commission.

Ball, S. (2003) The teacher's soul and the terrors of performativity, *Journal of Education Policy*, 18(2): 215–28.

Bandler, R. and Grinder, J. (1975) *The Structure of Magic.* Palo Alto, CA: Science and Behaviour Books.

Batmanghelidjh, C. (1999) Whose political correction? The challenge of therapeutic work with inner-city children experiencing deprivation, *Psychodynamic Counselling*, 5(2): 231–43.

Batmanghelidjh, C. (2006) *Shattered Lives: Children Who Live With Courage and Dignity.* London: Jessica Kingsley.

Becher, T. (1989) *Academic Tribes and Territories: Intellectual Enquiry and the Culture of Disciplines.* Milton Keynes: Society for Research into Higher Education and Open University Press.

Beek, C. (2002) The distribution of resources to support inclusive learning. *Support for Learning*, 17(1): 9–14.

Beveridge Report (1942) *Social Insurance and Allied Services*, Cmnd. 6404. London: HMSO.

Blow, K. (1994) Old chestnuts roasted in systemic consultancy with teachers, in C. Hampden-Turner, H. Brunning, D. Campbell, R. Draper and C. Huffington (eds) *Internal Consultancy in the Public Sector: Case Studies.* London: Karnac Books, pp. 145–59.

Buchanan, M. (2002) *Small World: Uncovering Nature's Hidden Networks.* London: Phoenix.

Burke, C. and Grosvenor, I. (2005) *The School I'd Like.* London: RoutledgeFalmer.

Cade, L. and Caffyn, R. (1994) 'The King Edward VI family: an example of clustering in Nottinghamshire, *Support for Learning*, 9(2): 83–8.

Cade, L. and Caffyn, R. (1995) Family planning for special needs: the role of a Nottinghamshire family special needs co-ordinator, *Support for Learning*, 10(2): 70–4.

Capra, F. (1996) *The Web of Life: A New Synthesis of Mind and Matter*. London: HarperCollins.

Chaffin, M. (2006) Organizational culture and practice epistemologies, *Clinical Psychology: Science and Practice*, 13(1): 90–3.

Checkland, P. and Scholes, J. (1999) *Soft Systems Methodology in Action*. London: John Wiley and Sons.

Crozier, G. and Reay, D. (eds) (2005) *Activating Participation: Parents and Teachers Working Towards Partnership*. Stoke-on-Trent: Trentham Books.

CYPB (Children and Young People's Board) (2007) *Oxfordshire Children and Young People's Survey 2007*. Oxford: Research Insight.

Dessent, T. (1988) *Making the Ordinary School Special*. London: Falmer Press.

DES (1985) *Better Schools*. London: HMSO.

Dewey, J. (1897) My pedagogic creed, *The School Journal*, 16 Jan., LIV(3).

Dewey, J. ([1900/43] 1990) *The School and Society: The Child and the Curriculum*, Chicago: University of Chicago Press.

DfEE (1997) *Excellence for All Children: Meeting Special Educational Needs*. London: HMSO.

DfEE (1998) *Excellence in Cities*. London: HMSO.

DfES (2004) *Every Child Matters: Change for Children*. Nottingham: HMSO.

DfES (2005) *Youth Matters*. Nottingham: HMSO.

DfES (2006a) *Youth Matters: Next Steps*. Nottingham: HMSO.

DfES (2006b) Reinforcing parental responsibility: parent support advisers, press release, 17 March available from the Government News Network at: www.gnn.gov.uk (accessed 10 Oct. 2007).

Dowling, E. and Osbourne, E. (1994) *The Family and the School: A Joint Systems Approach to Problems with Children*. London: Routledge.

Edwards, R. (ed.) (2002) *Children, Home and School: Regulation, Autonomy or Connection?* London: RoutledgeFalmer.

End Child Poverty (2007) Available at: www.endchildpoverty.org.uk (accessed 20 Oct. 2007).

Exeter Youth Support Team (1992) A model of Juvenile Liaison. Unpublished paper, Exeter Youth Support Team, Exeter.

Flecknoe, M. (2001) Target setting: will it help to raise achievement? *Educational Management and Administration*, 29(2): 217–28.

Freeman, P. (1999) Recursive politics: prevention, modernity and social systems, *Children and Society*, 13: 232–41.

Frost, N. (2005) *Professionalism, Partnership and Joined Up Thinking*. Dartington: Research in Practice.

Galloway, D. and Goodwin, C. (1987) *The Education of Disturbing Children: Pupils with Learning and Behaviour Difficulties*. London: Longman.

Gilligan, C. (1982) *In a Different Voice: Psychological Theory and Women's Development*. Cambridge, MA: Harvard University Press.

Gill, K. and Pickles, T. (eds) (1989) *Active Collaboration: Joint Practice and Youth Strategies*. Glasgow: Intermediate Treatment Resource Centre.

Glenny, G. (2000) *Thame Children and Young Persons' Interagency Network: Evaluation of Projects Funded by the Calouste Gulbenkian Foundation. February 2000*. Available at: www.brookes.ac.uk/schools/education/staffinfo/glenny.html (accessed 10 Feb. 2008).

Glenny, G. (2001) *Hamilton Oxford Schools Partnership, Integrated Support Services: Evaluation Report October 2001*. Available at: www.brookes.ac.uk/schools/education/staffinfo/glenny.html (accessed 10 Feb. 2008).

Glenny, G., in consultation with Godfrey, M. (2005a) *Oxfordshire Integrated Support Services Pilot: Evaluation Report, November 2005*. Available at: www.brookes.ac.uk/schools/education/staffinfo/glenny.html (accessed 10 Feb. 2008).

Glenny, G. (2005b) Riding the dragon: exploring the principles that underpin effective interagency networking, *Support for Learning*, 20(4): 167–75.

Glenny, G. (2007a) *The Home School Community Link Worker Project, Supported by Oxfordshire Children's Fund: Evaluation Report, May 2007*. Available at www.brookes.ac.uk/schools/education/staffinfo/glenny.html (accessed 10 Feb. 2008).

Glenny, G. (2007b) *The Identification and Support Service Project Supported by Oxfordshire Children's Fund: Evaluation Report, December 2007*. Available at: www.brookes.ac.uk/schools/education/staffinfo/glenny.html (accessed 10 Feb. 2008).

Glenny, G. and Lown, J. (1987) A follow up study of children returning to an integrated setting after placement in a language unit, with particular reference to the decision making processes of the professionals involved. Unpublished MSc dissertation, held in the library of the University of Sheffield, Sheffield.

Glenny, G. and Mannion, G. (2005) Inter-agency working for inclusive communities, *Support for Learning*, 20(4): 155–6.

Goldratt, E. M. (1990) *What is this Thing Called the Theory of Constraints and How Should it be Implemented?* Great Barrington, MA: North River Press.

Goldratt, E. M. (2006) *The Haystack Syndrome: Sifting Information out of the Data Ocean*. Great Barrington, MA: North River Press.

Gray, P. and Dessent, T. (1993) Getting our act together, *British Journal of Special Education*, 20(1): 9–11.

Gulaboff, D. (1989) The M.A.R.S. project in Dundee, in K. Gill and T. Pickles (eds) *Active Collaboration: Joint Practice and Youth Strategies*. Glasgow: Intermediate Treatment Resource Centre, pp. 30–8.

Handy, C. (1990) *Inside Organizations*. Harmondsworth: Penguin Books.

Harrison, J. and Bullock, J. (2005) Interagency approaches to the development of a school based student health service, *Support for Learning*, 20(4): 190–4.

Hemmelgarn, A. L., Glissen, C. and James, L. R. (2006) Organizational culture and climate: implications for services and interventions research, *Clinical Psychology: Science and Practice*, 13(1): 73–89.

Hodgkin, R. and Newell, P. (1996) *Effective Government Structures for Children: Report of a Gulbenkian Foundation Inquiry* London: Calouste Gulbenkian Foundation.

Holland, J. H. (1998) *Emergence: from Chaos to Order*. Oxford: Oxford University Press..

Hoxhallari, L., Conolly, A. and Lyon, N. (2007) *Families with Children in Britain: Findings from the 2005 Family and Children Study (FACS)*. London: Department for Work and Pensions.

Huxham, C. and Vangen, S. (2005) *Managing to Collaborate: The Theory and Practice of Collaborative Advantage*. London: Routledge.

Illsley, P. and Redford, M. (2005) 'Drop in for coffee': working with parents in North Perth Community School, *Support for Learning*, 20(4): 157–66.

Janis, I. L. (1972) *Victims of Groupthink: A Psychological Study of Foreign-Policy Decisions and Fiascos*. Boston: Houghton Mifflin Company.

Kauffman, S. A. (1993) *The Origins of Order: Self-organization and Selection in Evolution*. Oxford: Oxford University Press.

Kauffman, S. A. (1995a) *At Home in the Universe: The Search for the Laws of Self-organization and Complexity*. Oxford: Oxford University Press.

Kauffman, S. A. (1995b) Escaping the Red Queen effect, *The McKinsey Quarterly*, 1: 118–29.

Kelly, G. (1955) *The Psychology of Personal Construct Psychology*. New York: Norton.

Kilbrandon Report (1964) *The Report of the Committee on Children and Young Persons in Scotland*, Cmnd. 2306. Edinburgh: HMSO.

Laming Report (2003) *The Victoria Climbe Inquiry*. London: HMSO.

Lewin, R. (1993) *Complexity: Life at the Edge of Chaos*. Chicago: Chicago University Press.

Lindsay, G., Band, S., Cullen, M.A., et al. (2007) *Parental Support Advisor Pilot*, Research Report DCSF-RW020. London: Department for Children, Schools and Families.

Lundt, I., Evans, J., Norwich, B. and Wedell, K. (1994) *Working Together: Interschool Collaboration for Special Needs*. London: David Fulton Publishers.

Malaguzzi, L. (1993) History, ideas and basic philosophy, in C. Edwards, L. Gandini and G. Foreman (eds) *The Hundred Languages of Children*. Norwood, NJ: Ablex.

Maginnis, E. (1989) Lothian Region's youth strategy: a political perspective, in K. Gill and T. Pickles (eds) *Active Collaboration: Joint Practice and Youth Strategies*. Glasgow: Intermediate Treatment Resource Centre, pp. 7–14.

Mapstone, E. (1983) *Crossing the Boundaries: New Directions in the Mental Health Services for Children and Young People in Scotland*. Edinburgh: HMSO.

Marion, R. (1999) *The Edge of Organization: Chaos and Complexity Theories of Formal Social Systems*. Thousand Oaks, CA: Sage.

McConnell, E. (1994) Wither or whither collaboration? *Support for Learning*, 9(2): 89–93.

Miller, C. and McNicholl, A. (2003) *Integrating Children's Services: Issues and Practice*. London: Office of Public Management.

Minuchin, S. (1974) *Families and Family Therapy*. London: Tavistock.

Moss, P. and Petrie, P. (1997) *Children's Services: Time for a New Approach*. London: Institute of Education University of London.

Moss, P. and Petrie, P. (2002) *From Children's Services to Children's Spaces: Public Policy, Children and Childhood*. London: RoutledgeFalmer.

Mott, G. (2004) *Children at the Heart: Vision into Action*, EMIE Report 84. Slough: NFER.

Muir, L. (1984) Teamwork, in M. R. Olsen (ed.) *Social Work and Mental Health*. London: Tavistock, pp. 68–176.

OECD (Organisation for Economic Co-operation and Development) (1995) *Children and Youth at Risk*. Paris: Centre for Educational Research and Innovation OECD.

O'Neill, O. (2002) *A Question of Trust: The BBC Reith Lectures*. Cambridge: Cambridge University Press.

Ofsted (2000) *Evaluating Educational Inclusion: Guidance for Inspectors and Schools*. London: Ofsted.

Ofsted (2005) *Every Child Matters: Framework for the Inspection of Children's Services*. Available at: www.ofsted.gov.uk (accessed on 30 Nov. 2007).

Olsen, M. R. (ed.) (1984) *Social Work and Mental Health*. London: Tavistock.

Owen, H. (1996) *Creating Top Flight Teams*. London: Kogan Page.

Partridge, A. (2005) Children and young people's involvement in public decision making, *Support for Learning*, 20(4): 181–9.

Payne, L. (2007) A 'Children's Government' in England and child impact assessment, *Children and Society*, 21: 470–5.

Percy-Smith, J. (2006) What works in strategic partnerships for children: a research review, *Children and Society*, 20: 313–23.

Petrie, P., Moss, P., Cameron, C., et al. (in press) *Working Together: Interprofessional Working in Multipurpose Children's Settings*. London: Thomas Coram Research Unit.

Power, M. (1997) *The Audit Society: Rituals of Verification*. Oxford: Oxford University Press.

Prior, D. and Paris, A. (2005) *Preventing Children's Involvement in Crime and Anti-Social Behaviour: A Literature Review*, Research Report 623. London.: Department for Education and Skills.

Prout, A. (2000) Children's participation: control and self-realisation in British late modernity, *Children and Society*, 14(4): 304–15.

Rihani, S. (2005) NHS: anarchy or perfection. Paper given at the First Interdisciplinary Conference on Complexity, at the University of Liverpool, September, 2005.

Rihani, S. and Geyer, R. (2001) Complexity: an appropriate framework for development, *Progress in Development Studies*, 1(3): 237–45.

Roaf, C. (2002) *Coordinating Services for Including Children and Young People: Joined up Action*. Buckingham: Open University Press.

Roaf, C. and Lloyd, C. (1995) Multiagency work with young people in difficulty, *Social Care Research Findings*, No. 68, June. York: Joseph Rowntree Foundation.

Robinson, R. M., Anning, A., Cottrell, D., Frost, N. and Green, J. M. (2004) *New Forms of Professional Knowledge in Multi-Agency Delivery of Services for Children (The MATch Project), Report to the ESRC*. Available at: http://esrcsocietytoday.ac.uk.

Russell, L. (1989) Strathclyde Region: the development of policies for working with young people at risk, in K. Gill and T. Pickles (eds) *Active Collaboration: Joint Practice and Youth Strategies*. Glasgow: Intermediate Treatment Resource Centre, pp. 20–9.

Rutter, M. and Madge, N. (1976) *Cycles of Disadvantage*. London: Heinemann.

Rutter, M. (1980) *Changing Youth in a Changing Society: Patterns of Adolescent Development and Disorder*. Cambridge, MA: Harvard University Press.

Sampson, O. C. (1980) *Child Guidance: Its History, Provenance and Future*, Occasional Papers 3(3). London: British Psychological Society, Division of Educational and Child Psychology.

Schumacher, E. F. (1974) *Small is Beautiful: A Study of Economics as if People Mattered*. London: Abacus, Sphere Books.

Sen, A. (1999*) Democracy as Freedom*. Oxford: Oxford University Press.

Sennett, R. (1998) *The Corrosion of Character: The Personal Consequences of Work in the New Capitalism*. New York: W. W. Norton.

Siraj-Blatchford, I., Clarke, K. and Needham, M. (2007) *The Team Around the Child: Multiagency Working in the Early Years.* Stoke-on-Trent: Trentham Books.

Stacey, R. D. (2001) *Complex Responsive Processes in Organizations: Learning and Knowledge Creation.* London: Routledge.

Surrey County Council (1992) *Youth Link.* Woking: Woking Youth Office.

Tanner, E., Welsh, E. and Lewis, J. (2006) The quality-defining process in early years services: a case study, *Children and Society,* 20: 4–16.

Tett, L. (2000) Excluded voices: class, culture, and family literacy in Scotland, *Journal of Adolescent and Adult Literacy,* 44(2): 122–8.

Tett, L. (2005) Inter-agency partnerships and Integrated Community Schools: a Scottish perspective, *Support for Learning,* 20(4): 157–61.

Tett, L., Munn, P., Blair, A., et al. (2001) Collaboration between schools and community education agencies in tackling social exclusion, *Research Papers in Education,* 16(1): 3–21.

Todd, L. (2007) *Partnerships for Inclusive Education: A Critical Approach to Collaborative Working.* London: Routledge.

Tomlinson, K. (2003) *Effective Interagency Working: A Review of the Literature and Examples from Practice.* Slough: NFER.

UNICEF (2007) *Child Poverty in Perspective: An Overview of Child Well-Being in Rich Countries,* Report Card 7. Florence: UNICEF Innocenti Research Centre.

Vickers, G. ([1965] 1995) *The Art of Judgement: A Study of Policy Making.* London: Sage Centenary Edition.

Vulliamy, G. and Webb, R. (1999) *Meeting Need and Challenging Crime in Partnership with Schools,* Research Findings 96. London: Home Office Research, Development and Statistics Directorate.

Warin, J. (2007) Joined up services for young children and their families: papering over the cracks or reconstructing the foundations? *Children and Society,* 21: 87–97.

Webb, R. and Vulliamy, G. (2004) *A Multi-Agency Approach to Reducing Disaffection and Exclusions from School,* Research Report RR568. London: Department for Education and Skills.

Index

DEVELOPING MULTIPROFESSIONAL TEAMWORK FOR INTEGRATED CHILDREN'S SERVICES

Angela Anning, David Cottrell, Nick Frost, Josephine Green and Mark Robinson

Multiprofessional practice in the delivery of services is a central government imperative in the UK and other countries. This book offers a practical resource to professionals charged with conceptualising, planning, implementing and evaluating multiprofessional practice in children's services. The book:

- Exemplifies what multiprofessional work looks like in practice
- Examines real dilemmas faced by professionals trying to make it work, and shows how these dilemmas can be resolved
- Considers lessons to be learnt, implications for practice and recommendations for making multiprofessional practice effective

Discussion of dilemmas facing multiprofessional teams include organising and managing multi-professional teams, supporting professionals as they learn to adapt to new roles and responsibilities, and learning how to share professional knowledge and expertise.

Featuring useful guidance, theoretical frameworks and evidence-based insights into practice, this book is a key resource for students on courses studying early childhood and families, as well as social workers, teachers, support workers in children's centres, family support workers, health workers, and managers of a range of children and youth services.

Contents: Part One: Researching and understanding multi-professional teams working with children – Working in a multi-professional world – Researching multi-professional teams – Organising and managing multi-professional teams – Part Two: Working and learning in a multi-professional team – Multi-professional perspectives on childhood – Changing roles and responsibilities in multi-professional teams – Sharing knowledge in the multi-professional workplace – Part Three: Planning, implementing and supporting multi-professional teams working with children – Making it work 1: Addressing key dilemmas – Making it work 2: Strategies for decision-making and service delivery – Taking multi-professional practice forward

2006 156pp

978-0-335-21978-0 (Paperback)   978-0-335-21979-7 (Hardback)

EARLY CHILDHOOD STUDIES
A Multiprofessional Perspective

Liz Jones, Rachel Holmes and John Powell

"Students and trainers, policy makers and practitioners have a duty to be knowledgeable, to be able to reflect on their beliefs and practice and to articulate concerns, share their views, convey their enthusiasm and act as advocates for young children. This book will help them do just that."
Lesley Abbott OBE, Mancester Metropolitan University

Early Childhood Studies critically engages the reader in issues that relate to young children and their lives from a multiprofessional perspective. Whilst offering a theoretically rigorous treatment of issues relating to early childhood studies, the book also provides practical discussion of strategies that could inform multiprofessional practice. It draws upon case studies to help the reader make practical sense of theoretical ideas and develop a critical and reflective attitude. Hard and pressing questions are asked so that beliefs, ideas, views and assumptions about notions of the child and childhood are constantly critiqued and reframed for the post-modern world.

The first part of the book explores the early years, power and politics by looking at child rights, the politics of play, families, and working with parents and carers. The second part explores facts and fantasies about childhood experiences, such as anti-discriminatory practice, the law, child protection, and health issues. The final section encourages the reader to explore what childhood means from historical, ideological and cultural perspectives, and looks at how popular assumptions arise.

This is a key critical text for early childhood students, academics and researchers, as well as practitioners who want to develop their reflective practice.

Contents: *List of Contributors – Foreword – Preface and acknowledgements – Introduction – Part 1: Power, politics and childhood – Researching young children within a multiprofessional perspective – Exploring tensions within the interplay of rights, duties and responsibilities – The politics of play – Exploring families – Working with parents and carers – Part 2: Working together: Facts, frameworks and fantasies – Multiprofessional perspectives – Anti-discriminatory practice – Legal issues – Child protection – Integration, inclusion and diversity – Health in childhood – Part 3: Children's childhoods – Exploring representations of children and childhood in history and film: Silencing a voice that is already blue in the face from shouting – Exploring representations of children and childhood in photography and documentary: Visualizing the silence – International perspectives – Understanding development – Concluding remarks – Index.*

2005 240pp

978-0-335-21485-3 (Paperback) 978-0-335-21486-0 (Hardback)

LEARNING FROM SURESTART
Working with Young Children and their Families

Jo Weinberger, Caroline Pickstone and Peter Hannon (eds)

"This book demonstrates the key strength of Sure Start, its breadth of vision... It shows how with the right effort, statutory and voluntary organisations can work side by side. It also shows how important it is to engage local people in finding solutions, blending professional and community support to strengthen both... Learning from Sure Start is a significant contribution to the evidence base on what works for young children and families."
Naomi Eisenstadt, Director, Sure Start Unit

Sure Start, an exciting initiative in early childhood care and education with families in the UK, has been developing new forms of community-focused early interventions, with the aim of having all children 'ready to flourish' when they start school.

This book, the first of its kind, is the result of a close collaboration between one local programme and a university over a five year period. The contributors all have first hand experience as practitioners or researchers in the Sure Start programme at Foxhill & Parson Cross in Sheffield, which has provided a wide range of new services. Contributors:

- Describe various services within health, education and social welfare
- Examine implications of the development of inter-agency theory and practice for planning and delivery of services for children
- Evaluate methods that were employed
- Identify what worked and what didn't
- Indicate lessons that can be drawn from experience

This is indispensable reading for students of early childhood and early years practitioners, policy makers, and researchers.

Contributors: Sue Battersby, Robin Carlisle, Deborah Crofts, Margaret Drake, Fiona Ford, Jan Forde, Linda Fox, Imogen Hale, Peter Hannon, Helen Lomas, Jackie Marsh, Anne Morgan, Simon Martinez, Caroline Pickstone, Ann Rowe, Jo Weinberger.

Contents: Foreword – Contributors – List of abbreviations – Part one: Introduction – Why we should learn from Sure Start – Listening to families: a survey of parents' views – Part two: Improving and emotional development – Family support – 'Connecting with our kids' parenting programme – Meeting the needs of teenage parents – Part three: Improving health – Low birth weight: Exploring the contribution of nutrition – Supporting breast feeding mothers – The impact of Sure Start on health visiting – Child safety scheme – Part four: Improving children's ability to learn – Quality of play and learning opportunities – Community teaching in a Sure Start context – Screening and language development – Media, popular culture and young children – A dialogic reading intervention programme for parents and preschoolers – Part five: Strengthening families and communities – Community involvement – The Young Families' Advice Service – Community research – Part six: What have we learned? What do we need to know? – Bringing it together: the role of the programme manager – Looking to the future – Appendices – Index.

2005 304pp

978-0-335-21638-3 (Paperback)   978-0-335-21639-0 (Hardback)